SINGAPORE
1942

SINGAPORE
1942

CHRIS BROWN

The
History
Press

First published 2012 by Spellmount
This edition first published 2022

The History Press
97 St George's Place, Cheltenham,
Gloucestershire, GL50 3QB
www.thehistorypress.co.uk

British Library Cataloguing in Publication Data.
A catalogue record for this book is available from the British Library.

ISBN 978 0 7509 9933 5

Typesetting and origination by The History Press
Printed and bound in Great Britain by TJ Books Limited, Padstow,
Cornwall.

MIX
Paper from
responsible sources
FSC   FSC® C013056
www.fsc.org

Trees for LYfe

CONTENTS

ACKNOWLEDGEMENTS

I have been interested in this battle since I was a boy living in Singapore in the mid-1960s when the campaign was still very fresh in the collective consciousness of the community. The events had occurred only twenty years previously. Although that seemed very distant to a child of 7 or 8, most of the adult population had lived through the Japanese occupation and the memory was regularly refreshed by the frequent discoveries of bodies when new building projects were breaking ground. This book does not aim to provide the reader with a definitive, detailed blow-by-blow account of the battles that occurred in February 1942; that would require a volume of several hundred pages. The intention is to provide an outline of the historical, economic and military environment surrounding the campaign.

As ever, writing this book would have been impossible without the support and encouragement of my wife, Pat, and my son, Robert, who has saved me from several computer disasters. I would also like to take this opportunity to express my gratitude to my parents, Revd Peter and Mrs Margaret Brown, to Robert and Rosina Walker of Dunfermline for their kindness, generosity and general interest in my well-being when I was a teenager, and to Jo de Vries of The History Press for her remarkable patience.

LIST OF ILLUSTRATIONS

35. Typical pre-war 'atap' house of the kind found in *kampongs* (villages) the length and breadth of Malaya and Singapore. (Author's collection)
36. Typical pre-war shop-houses of the kind found throughout Malaya and Singapore. (Author's collection)
37. Restored 6in gun position at the excellent Siloso Fort Museum, Sentosa, Singapore. (Author's collection)
38. Forest and mountain terrain in eastern Malaya. (Author's collection)
39. A jungle creek. Although few Japanese soldiers had received any jungle-warfare training, they proved adept at infiltrating Allied positions by following small streams like this one in western Singapore. (Author's collection)
40. Gen. Wavell in Singapore inspecting coastal guns, November 1941.
41. The Japanese victory parade in Fullerton Square, Singapore, 17 February 1942.
42. Lt Gen. Percival and party en route to surrender Singapore to the Japanese.
43. Rice country in eastern Malaya. Far from being covered by 'impenetrable jungle', a great deal of 1940s Malaya was agricultural land. (Author's collection)
44. One British pre-war banknote and three Japanese 'Occupation' currency banknotes. The Japanese banknotes lost their value very quickly during the occupation years. (Author's collection)

Maps

Malaya/Singapore Island. Location of military formations, airfields and air force units, 8 December 1941.
Withdrawal to Singapore.
Singapore Island dispositions.
Assault on Singapore.
Operations of 10 February 1942.
Operations of 11 February 1942.
Singapore town.

INTRODUCTION

The campaign in Malaya and the resulting fall of Singapore in February 1942 was not simply a product of the outbreak of the Second World War. A rising population and a stagnating economic base undermined the credibility of the imperial government and made war a possible means of ensuring stability at home and enhancing the status of Japan abroad, but Japan's road to war was not simply a matter of seizing an opportunity; it was also a product of being brought into the industrial age.

In 1549 Portuguese explorers landed at Tanegashima and were followed six years later by a Jesuit mission. Catholicism proved to be popular, but eventually the missions were seen as a troublesome influence and a threat to Japanese culture. By the 1620s Catholicism had been completely suppressed and for the next 200 years and more Japan maintained a policy of virtual isolation from the rest of the world. The period of *Sakoku* (exclusion) lasted until 1853, when an American naval force under Commodore Perry entered Yokohama. Throughout the 1850s Japan was forced to accept unequal treaties with the United States and various European powers. If Japan was to be able to protect herself from foreign pressure and interference, she needed to develop a strong national government and a powerful navy.

The first major modern warship of the Imperial Japanese Navy was the *Jo Sho Maru*. She was designed by Thomas Blake Glover, built at Aberdeen and delivered on 8 May 1870. This was the beginning of a long naval relationship between Britain and Japan; indeed an imperial decree of 1870 stipulated that the Royal Navy should be the model for the future development of the Imperial Navy. Japan flirted with the creation of a major navy throughout the 1870s, mounting expeditions to Taiwan and Korea.

Her naval development stalled due to a series of internal conflicts, but by the 1880s she had acquired several British- and French-built warships. The rise of Japan as maritime power in East Asia allowed her to force her will on China and Korea, and to make Taiwan a colony. In 1904 Japan went to war with Russia, decisively winning the great naval battle of Tsushima and confirming her status as a rising power at sea. Six years later Japan formally annexed Korea, an action that drew some criticism but no action from the rest of the world. Strange as it may seem now, this was not so very remarkable in 1910. European powers had already carved out colonies in Africa and Asia; why should Japan not do the same?

In August 1914 Britain sought Japanese aid against German commerce raiders operating around the coast of China, and Japan formally declared war on Germany on 23 August. Through the course of the war Japan extended her influence in China and undertook several operations against German possessions, forcing the surrender of Tsingtao and launching the first ever aerial bombardment from ships.

From a Japanese perspective, supporting the Entente Allies (Britain, France and America) in the First World War had not brought them either respect or power. Japanese industry flourished in the war years, but her market share dwindled thereafter. The ensuing recession was to become a major factor in promoting a form of ultra-nationalist militarism and driving an ambition to form an empire in Asia which could provide her with raw materials and a captive market. The terms of the Washington Conference on arms limitation struck a blow at national self-respect by limiting Japanese warship construction, which in turn impaired the viability of her shipbuilding industry. This caused unemployment that was blamed on the Washington Conference powers, though in fact Japan was struggling economically anyway.

The expansion of the Japanese Empire took a further step in September 1931 with the invasion of Manchuria. In due course a puppet state – Manchukuo – was erected, headed by the last Emperor of China, Pu-Yi. Unlike the invasion of Korea in 1910, the Manchurian campaign provoked some reaction around the world and prompted the League of Nations to send a commission of inquiry. Reports of atrocities against civilians and prisoners, though dismissed as fabrications by Japan, were widely accepted elsewhere, and in February 1933 Japan resigned from the League of Nations in protest against criticism of her actions in Manchuria.

At the start of the Second World War Britain, France, the Netherlands and the United States controlled the majority of South East Asia; even Portugal retained colonies at Macau and East Timor.

The German conquest of France and the Netherlands in 1940 made their colonies in what are now Vietnam, Laos, Cambodia and Indonesia very vulnerable since there was no longer any prospect of support from the home country. The perilous situation of Britain had similar implications for Malaya, Singapore, Hong Kong and Burma. The weakness of the colonial powers was an important factor in deciding the direction and timing of Japan's incredibly daring series of offensives in December 1941, but in fact she was already at war in China. In a sense, she was simply opening several new fronts at once.

Initially, the emphasis had been on the annexation of Manchuria; the provocative actions that sparked expansion into China were manufactured by the Imperial Army as what we might call 'private enterprise', though at the time the military was the dominant force in all aspects of Japanese political life.

International reaction to the Sino-Japanese war was both a direct and indirect factor in taking Japan to war with the colonial powers. Various trade sanctions, most significantly in relation to oil and scrap metal from America, had a detrimental effect on the economy and were perceived, perhaps understandably, as insulting since no European power would have been treated in the same way. At the same time, it further separated Japan from the wider political and diplomatic community. Even so, whilst all of the issues that arose in the 1920s and 1930s contributed to the invasions of 1941, the real foundations of what Japanese historians call the Great East Asian War or the Pacific War had been laid long before.

TIMELINE

1933	Japan annexes Manchuria and leaves the League of Nations.
1934	Japan disregards the existing disarmament treaties.
1935	Japan withdraws from the London Naval Conference to pursue developing a larger navy than that allowed by the Washington Conference.
1937	Japan invades China and seizes Nanking, where Japanese troops commit widespread atrocities on the inhabitants.
1939	Completion of the Singapore naval base at Sembawang.
1940	Japan forces the pro-Vichy government of French Indo-China to accept Japanese troops and airfields.
2 December	Japanese naval units ordered to move to their positions for the attacks on Hawaii, Malaya, Thailand and Hong Kong.
6 December	Japanese transport ships are seen approaching Malaya.
7 December	The Japanese attack on Pearl Harbor sinks or damages eight US battleships and destroys nearly 200 aircraft.

1941

1941

7/8 December	At night, Singapore subjected to air raids killing 200 people and damaging the RAF airfields at Tengah and Seletar.
8 December	Hong Kong attacked overland through the 'New Territories' and Japanese landing takes place to the north of Kota Bahru in north-east Malaya.
10 December	HMS *Prince of Wales* and HMS *Repulse* sunk by Japanese torpedo bombers operating from French Indo-China (modern-day Vietnam); Albert 'Duff' Cooper appointed as Resident Minister for Far Eastern Affairs.
11/12 December	British and Indian troops are defeated at Jitra in northern Malaya.
14/15 December	British and Indian troops are defeated at Gurun, forcing the evacuation of the state of Kedah.
16/17 December	Penang evacuated.
25 December	Hong Kong falls to the Japanese.

1942

3 January	Arrival of 45th Indian Brigade in Singapore, the first body of reinforcements since the start of the campaign.
7 January	British and Indian forces are defeated at Slim River.
11 January	Kuala Lumpur falls to the Japanese.
15 January	General Wavell assumes command of the ABDA (American, British, Dutch and Australian) forces in the south-west Pacific.
26 January	General Heath issues instructions for the withdrawal of III Corps from Johore to Singapore Island through the night of 31 January/1 February.
27 January	Percival receives permission to withdraw all Malaya Command troops to Singapore at his discretion.

Timeline

1942

31 January/ 1 February	Withdrawal to Singapore completed and part of the causeway destroyed.
7/8 February	Japanese troops seize Pulau Ubin in the Johore Strait.
8 February	First Japanese troops land on Singapore Island.
15 February	Percival holds his final conference at Fort Canning and decides to surrender.

HISTORICAL BACKGROUND

As one of the Allies during the First World War, Japan had some right to feel that she had not benefitted from the spoils of victory. Other than a few marginal gains from the defunct German Empire, Japan had little to show for her involvement in the greatest war of all time. Although her direct participation had been much less of a burden than that of France, Britain or the United States, Japan's contribution was not marginal. Her extensive naval assets had been deployed throughout the Pacific, the South China Sea and the Indian Ocean. They had thus relieved the British and the French – and to a lesser extent the Americans – from the task of protecting Far Eastern trade routes from German commerce raiders and therefore allowed production and export to continue with little interruption.

The diplomatic arrangements that emerged after 1919 did nothing to assuage Japanese sentiment. The arms control policies agreed at the Washington Conference put severe constraints on the construction of major warships, particularly battleships, which were still seen as the prime weapon at sea. Events would show that the nature of naval warfare had changed, and that the future of naval warfare really lay with the bombs and torpedoes that could be deployed from an aircraft carrier rather than the massive guns of battleships, but this was not yet apparent in the 1920s. Even so,

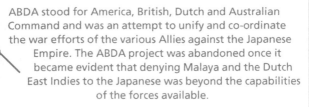

ABDA

ABDA stood for America, British, Dutch and Australian Command and was an attempt to unify and co-ordinate the war efforts of the various Allies against the Japanese Empire. The ABDA project was abandoned once it became evident that denying Malaya and the Dutch East Indies to the Japanese was beyond the capabilities of the forces available.

the fact that under the Washington Conference agreement Japan was limited to having only a proportion of the number of major warships allowed to either Britain, France or the United States was, understandably, seen as insulting. Although the other Allies could reasonably argue that they had commitments all round the world whereas Japan's interests were largely focused on the Pacific, there was a clear implication that the Western Allies had combined to ensure that Japan was to be restricted to being a second-tier maritime power.

This was particularly galling in relation to Britain and France, since a significant part of their justification for having large fleets was their need to protect their colonial and imperial interests, some of which – and a commercially significant proportion at that – lay in South Asia. Like Japan, France and Britain were primarily manufacturing economies with banking and insurance sectors that were built on their overseas trade. That trade, in turn, depended on the position of enterprises that could enjoy a preferential position on the markets of British and French colonies. Imperialist expansion gave Britain, France and the Netherlands a stranglehold on the exports of South Asia, but also gave them a more or less captive market. Japanese expansion in Korea and Manchuria was more focused on acquiring raw materials that could be consumed at home or be turned into finished products for export around the world than on building markets within the imperial domain, but the emperor's government saw no good reason why Japan should not enjoy the power, privileges and prestige of acquiring a network of colonial possessions. If it was good enough for the British, the French and the Dutch, it was good enough for Japan. The role of the United States in South Asia might seem a little different superficially, since there was no intention to retain the Philippines as a permanent, formal colony, but that probably seemed to be a distinction without a difference in Tokyo.

The Japanese conquest of Manchuria was met with condemnation from all sides, but given the position of the Western powers, there was more than a whiff of hypocrisy involved and since nobody was willing to go to the aid of Manchuria there was little to discourage Japan from actively pursuing an expansionist policy if the opportunity arose.

Political opinion in Japan was divided by two possible approaches to expansion. Some favoured a northern strategy to exploit the natural and human resources of Korea (which had been conquered by Japan) and Manchuria to help further the war in China, while others favoured a southern strategy aimed at seizing the tin, rubber and agricultural produce of Thailand and Malaya, and the rubber and timber of the Dutch East Indies and Burma. Each prospect had its merits. A protracted war would require vast quantities of oil, rubber and tin, which, realistically, could only come from South Asia, thus giving economic aid to Britain, France and the Netherlands just when they were at their weakest. Since the successful German occupation of northern Europe in 1940 there was little prospect of the French or Dutch colonial forces being reinforced. On the other hand, it was possible that Japan could continue to extend its occupation in China without provoking a war with Britain or the United States. The shortage of raw materials for Japanese industry was exacerbated by trade sanctions, particularly on oil and a ban on the export of scrap metal from the United States. Individually, none of these factors need necessarily have led to war, but a strong body of ultra-nationalist opinion certainly encouraged the possibility. The question of adopting a southern or northern strategy was not, initially, settled by the outbreak of war in Europe in 1939. The Phoney War period from September that year to May 1940 did not reveal the weakness of the Western powers, but the campaign through Belgium, the Netherlands and France most certainly did. Within a matter of weeks, the Netherlands and France had been utterly defeated and the British Army driven out of mainland Europe with a tremendous loss of materiel was clearly unable to divert significant quantities of men or materiel to Asia. The fall of France put the colonial government of French Indo-China (modern-day Vietnam) in a difficult position. They were in no position to resist demands from the Japanese government given that their own country was now under the control of Japan's ally, Germany. This would prove to be a significant factor once the war erupted in Asia since Japanese aircraft based in Indo-China would be able to mount operations as far south as Singapore.

Although economic factors were critical in the development of Japan's route to war with the Western powers, there was also a political dimension. In December 1938 Fumimaro Konoe, the Japanese prime minister, declared a policy titled the 'New Order in East Asia' which would encourage the growth of an economic area dominated by the Yen rather than the currencies of Europe. Initially intended as a development in the northern portions of East Asia, the 'New Order' was the foundation of the 'greater East Asia Co-Prosperity Sphere'; essentially a catch-all phrase to cover all of the territory that fell under Japanese domination. Although the Co-Prosperity Sphere concept was largely a fig leaf to disguise Japanese imperial expansion, there was a degree of wider political idealism involved. One of the slogans of the supporters of scheme was 'Asia for the Asiatics' and there was, to a modest extent, a genuine ambition to destroy European and American colonialist power throughout South Asia, though in reality this was largely a matter of seeking to replace European hegemony with Japanese political and economic domination. To some extent the development of the Co-Prosperity Sphere policy was a reaction to racialist policies among the Western powers. In 1919 the Japanese delegation to the Versailles treaty negotiations had proposed a declaration of universal racial equality. This was vetoed by President Woodrow Wilson – though he had no right to do so – because it would undermine the position of the colonial powers which had emerged victorious from the First World War and which had extensive interests in Asia, South America and Africa. It might have also caused him considerable political difficulty at home, given the strong tradition of racialist policies and practices in many American states; this was, after all, a time when the leaders of the Ku Klux Klan could still be received formally at the White House.

Naturally, some people in the nations conquered by Japan in 1941–42 saw the removal of British and Dutch colonial governments as a step toward national independence, and the Co-Prosperity Sphere concept as a possible route to economic development that would benefit their own communities rather than corporations in Britain and the Netherlands. Any such hopes were quickly undermined by the nature of the Japanese occupations and it rapidly became all too clear that the removal of one set of colonial masters meant nothing more than the installation of a different foreign power. However, in some locations in Malaya and a little more widely in the Dutch East Indies the Japanese were not, initially, regarded with total suspicion and some Japanese soldiers genuinely thought they were engaged in a war to liberate their fellow Asians from European and American imperialism.

The German conquest of France and the Netherlands in 1940 and the continuing troubles of the British through early 1941 presented Japan with an opportunity to remove European influence from Asia and to become the undisputed major power in the East. This could only be achieved if the United States could be neutralised. In late 1941 America was not yet prepared for a major war, but was certainly moving in that direction. The British were starting to make a modest degree of recovery in their campaigns against Germany and Italy, but were still struggling to maintain imports across the Atlantic from America and, after the summer of 1941, had the added burden of making a contribution to the Russian front as well. If a victory was to be gained, Japan had to make a move before the American military could be put on a real war footing and before the British improved sufficiently on their current situation to give serious attention to matters in the Far East. If the blow was to be struck at all, it had to be struck quickly and at all of the opposing powers at the same time to prevent one coming to the aid of the other. The Japanese offensive of December 1941 delivered just such a blow; it was incredibly audacious and an absolute masterpiece of planning and military ingenuity; for a while it achieved the political objective of Japanese primacy throughout the Far East. The seaborne landings mounted in Malaya and south Thailand were only part of a much wider picture and although the strike against Pearl Harbor inflicted a grave injury on the American Pacific Fleet, the blow was far from fatal. When the Japanese attack hit Pearl Harbor there were no American aircraft carriers in port. This would turn out to be a matter of huge consequence, but that was not altogether clear at the time.

There were other, less dramatic factors in leading Japan to adopt a war policy. The conflict in China had not been as swift or as straightforward as had been anticipated. One of the political justifications for attacking the British and the Americans was that both powers would be forced to reduce their support for the Chiang Kai-shek's forces. This was less than realistic since Chiang was much more reliant on support from the Soviet Union, but it did have a certain appeal to popular opinion in Japan and the news media – totally under Japanese government control – encouraged the belief that the Chinese forces would be mortally weakened by the loss of American aid. Similarly, there was a view that the Chinese government was heavily reliant on the fundraising activities of the Chinese diaspora of merchants and professionals across South Asia generally, but in Singapore and Malaya in particular. This was not unfounded; the Chinese communities did raise substantial sums for the war effort at home, but certainly not enough to have a profound effect on China's ability to resist the Japanese invasion. In reality, fundraising in the British colonies and American contributions to the Chinese government were insignificant issues compared to the wider questions of Japan's economic need for raw materials and foodstuffs, as well as her political desire to be a great international power and the leading force in Asia; neither issue – singly or in combination – was enough of a challenge to provoke war.

The attacks of December 1941 brought the Western Allies together with a shared objective: the defeat of Japan. In the early months of the war active co-operation was almost non-existent. The United States was not in a position to intervene in support of Britain or the Netherlands; although America had been providing arms and other supplies to Britain for some considerable time, the tide of public opinion in the US had not turned in favour of active participation. Pearl Harbor changed everything in that regard. America had been attacked with no declaration of war, thousands of lives and millions of dollars' worth of material had been destroyed and the American public was now ready for a fight even if their military was not. In that sense, the Pearl Harbor attack can be seen as a gigantic political and strategic error. It is not absolutely certain that the United States would have entered a war with Japan on the basis of her invasions of Malaya and the Dutch East Indies, but there could be little doubt that a direct attack on an American port or on the Philippines would force the issue.

Japan's attack on America did more than bring war to the Pacific. Germany chose to declare war on the United States in support of her Asian ally. President Roosevelt had been pushing toward declaring war with Germany for some time, but had not had the political support which would enable him to do so; now Hitler had saved him the necessity by declaring war on the United States.

In a sense, this clearly defined who was fighting for what. At its simplest, the Western Allies were committed to a war which would destroy the power of Germany, Japan and Italy, and in turn

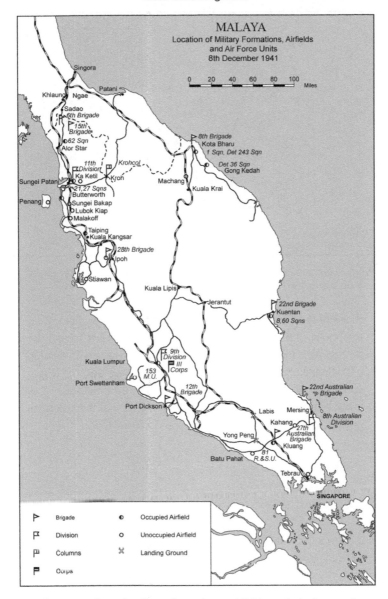

Malaya. Location of military formations, airfields and air force units, 8 December 1941.

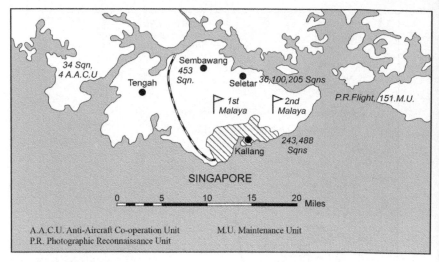

Singapore 1942

34 Sqn, 4 A.A.C.U

Tengah

Sembawang
453 Sqn.

Seletar 36,100,205 Sqns

1st Malaya

2nd Malaya

P.R.Flight, 151.M.U.

Kallang

243,488 Sqns

SINGAPORE

0   5   10   15   20 Miles

A.A.C.U. Anti-Aircraft Co-operation Unit   M.U. Maintenance Unit
P.R. Photographic Reconnaissance Unit

Singapore Island. Location of military formations, airfields and air force units, 8 December 1941.

those nations were committed to a war which would destroy the power of Britain and America. In the case of Britain and the Netherlands, this included ensuring that they retained possession of the mineral and agricultural wealth of Malaya and the Dutch East Indies. They could only do this by preserving a certain aura of invincibility and convincing local public opinion that the European powers could protect their communities from invasion.

THE ARMIES

The British Defence

The British defence posture in Malaya was bound by several constraints, some of which were effectively contradictory. Both Malaya and the Dutch East Indies had long been seen as military backwaters. Despite the economic significance of South East Asia to both Britain and the Netherlands, neither country had really made any great effort to ensure that there was proper planning and organisational procedures in the pre-war years. From the 1920s onward, successive British governments had developed a policy of simply assuming that there would not be another major war for the next ten years; a policy that was renewed periodically by incoming governments as they tried to cope with the depression of the 1930s by limiting spending on defence. The huge investment in the Singapore naval base would be the great exception, but in practice the failure to provide the necessary structure to protect the base would in due course make it something of a white elephant. The base was not simply a military asset. In part it was built to show the power of the British Empire and to demonstrate an intention to retain control of the Far East colonies, and thus the mineral wealth of Malaya and the commercial value of Singapore. It was also a gesture of solidarity with Australia and New Zealand; an indication that Britain was committed to ensuring the viability of the trade routes through the Pacific, the Indian Ocean and the South China Sea.

It was also a statement aimed at Japan: that Britain intended to be the primary naval power in the Western Pacific in partnership with the United States in the Central and Eastern Pacific. Naturally, such a policy rested on having a powerful and modern fleet that would be the equal of any Japanese force. Since Britain could not possibly hope to maintain such a fleet at Singapore without abandoning her commitments elsewhere, the statement was less than secure, but the British government felt confident – and with some reason – that in the event of a war with Japan, they would be able to count on American support. Planning for war in South East Asia essentially depended on the belief that Singapore could stand for 180 days, the maximum length of time that it would take to mount a relief expedition. In fact, the necessary stockpile of supplies was never amassed and the plan had not taken account of the possibility that there might be a major war in Europe that would prevent the dispatch of ships and materiel to Singapore. Defeat in the East was not inevitable even as late as 1939, and it was not unreasonable that the reality of war with Germany and Italy should take precedence over the possibility of war with Japan. There was little value in preserving distant colonies if the home country was at risk of being conquered. Equally, there was no value to maintaining a very large force of men on the other side of the world if they were not to be equipped properly, trained properly or led properly, and the failure to put sensible policies in place in any of these regards was an inexcusable dereliction of duty on the part of both the civil and military power in London.

The planning process of the 1930s depended on a large air force and a consequent need to protect the many airfields scattered through the peninsula, but there were also political and diplomatic considerations. British rule in Malaya had not been achieved through simple conquest and there was no single unified system of political control. The Straits Settlements – Singapore, Dinding

1. *Scottish company of the Federated Malay States Volunteers. (Malayan Volunteers Association)*

and Penang – constituted a single Crown colony, but the rest of Malaya fell into two groups, the Federated Malay States (FMS) of Pahang, Perak, Negri Sembilan and Selangor and the Unfederated Malay States of Terengganu, Perlis, Johore, Kedah and Kelantan. The latter group enjoyed a greater degree of self-government than the others, but the British administration was obliged to provide defence for all of them. The rapid advance of the Japanese effectively rendered the treaty obligations redundant, but they had only exerted a very minor influence on the general planning process. Although there was clearly little he could do, throughout the course of the campaign Lieutenant General Arthur Percival, General Officer Commanding (GOC) of Malaya Command, would receive a number of remonstrations from sultans who felt, not unreasonably, that the British were failing to live up to their obligations.

In practical military terms, Percival's chief responsibilities were the defence of Malaya as a valuable economic asset and that was seen as depending on, and being crucial to, the preservation of the

2. Wartime medical pannier, possibly issued to the Federated Malay States Volunteers. (Author's collection)

3. A pre-war elevated bungalow in the Singapore naval base. (Author's collection)

massive Singapore naval base. Construction of the base had been announced in 1923 but progress had been slow until the Japanese attack on Manchuria in 1931. By the time it was completed in 1939 it had cost something in the region of £60 million and was possibly the most costly naval installation ever built. It covered more than 20 square miles, held a massive fuel supply and had the largest dry dock in the world. It was built to support a massive fleet which could protect British interests throughout Asia, the Indian Ocean and the Pacific, but by the time hostilities began in 1941 Britain was already at war with Germany and Italy and most of the fleet was already committed to operations in the Atlantic and the Mediterranean, thus little could be spared for operations in South Asia.

Arthur Percival

Born in 1887, Percival joined the army on the first day of the First World War as a private soldier. After a short spell in basic training he was selected for a temporary commission and had been promoted to captain before the end of the year. By mid-1916 he had transferred to the regular army and was commissioned as captain in the Essex Regiment. He proved to be an effective, conscientious and courageous officer, and he rose to command a battalion and, for a short time in 1918, a brigade. At the end of the war he volunteered for the Archangel Command of the British Military Mission and thereafter served in Ireland where he was the target of two IRA assassination attempts. After passing out from Camberley Staff College, where he made a good impression on the faculty, he was selected for a scheme of accelerated promotion that was designed to undermine the army tradition of 'buggins turn', which was – rightly – seen by many as an impediment to good practice. He spent four years as a staff officer in West Africa and, after a spell at the Royal Naval College, Greenwich, returned to Camberley as an instructor.

Between 1936 and 1938 he served as a senior staff officer with Malaya Command and identified several of the weaknesses of

the situation. He wrote a paper illustrating the means by which Singapore could be attacked overland from Thailand and was acutely aware of the shortage of defensive installations on the northern shore of the island. Despite this knowledge, a mixture of financial stringencies and civil obstruction prevented him from doing very much to rectify those problems when he was appointed as GOC Malaya Command in April 1941; in fact, he actively opposed building fortifications on the northern shore of Singapore Island on the grounds that they would be bad for morale.

There was nothing he could do to persuade the government in London that Malaya Command needed adequate armoured vehicles and, although he was aware that the policy of defending airfields throughout the peninsula was utterly compromised by the shortage of suitable aircraft, he did not act to overturn the policy. Similarly, he remained focused on the necessity of protecting the great Singapore naval base at Sembawang long after it became redundant through the loss of Force Z at the beginning of the campaign. Percival spent the years 1942 to 1945 as a prisoner of war in Taiwan and Manchuria, and after the war he was active on behalf of FEPOW, the Far East Prisoners of War Association.

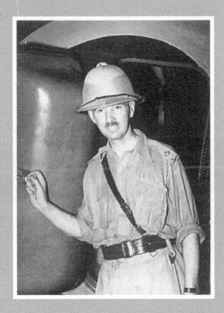

Opposite: 4. Lt Gen. Percival with war correspondents shortly before capitulation in Singapore, late January 1942.

5. Lt Gen. Percival on arrival in Singapore as the new GOC Malaya.

HMS *PRINCE OF WALES*

Weighing over 37,000 tons, armed with ten 14in guns and with a top speed of over 28 knots (32mph), HMS *Prince of Wales* was one of the most modern battleships in the world, but the day of the battleship was long past. She was launched in May 1939 and was not yet complete when the war started. She came close to being destroyed in a German air raid in 1940 while she was still being fitted out. She was in action against the *Bismarck* and suffered damage which was repaired at Rosyth before being assigned to transport the prime minister, Winston Churchill, to a conference with President Roosevelt. On 10 December 1941 she was attacked by Japanese 'Betty' torpedo bombers, with the loss of over 300 of her 1,500-man crew. *Prince of Wales* and *Repulse* were the first warships of their respective classes (battleship and battlecruiser) to be sunk by aircraft while at sea. American and Italian ships had been sunk by air power whilst in port at Taranto and Pearl Harbor.

6. *HMS* Prince of Wales.

Although there was a general reluctance to accept that there would be war with Japan, it was decided that a strong naval presence in Singapore might act as a deterrent and that the force of one heavy cruiser, four light cruisers (of First World War vintage) and three destroyers currently based at Singapore should be reinforced with the battleship *Prince of Wales* and the battlecruiser *Repulse*. A plan to supplement the force with the aircraft carrier *Indomitable* had to be abandoned when she ran aground near Jamaica. *Repulse*, *Prince of Wales* and four destroyers – known collectively as 'Force Z' – arrived in Singapore on 2 December 1941, only a week before the Japanese landings. The arrival of Force Z was a boost to the confidence of the British establishment and played well in the local press, but the absence of an aircraft carrier would prove to be a great weakness when battle was joined.

British Air Strength

The naval base was a significant military and political asset, but it was not a fortification and was not defensible in isolation. As early as 1940, Percival's predecessor as GOC Malaya Command – Lt Gen. Lionel Bond – was well aware that Singapore could not be held securely without possession of the rest of Malaya, and that this could not be achieved without a strong army and, crucially, large numbers of aircraft.

The airfields to support an extensive air force had already been built, but the demands of the other theatres meant that only a small number – and none of the more advanced models – could be spared for Malaya. At the time of the Japanese attack there was a total of only 158 RAF aircraft in the region, although it had been suggested as early as October 1940 that a force of nearly 600 front-line aircraft was required. In addition to being woefully understrength in quantity, the RAF presence was also of poor quality. Only one-third of the aircraft in front-line service were fighters; all of them Brewster Buffaloes. The Buffalo suffered from

BREWSTER BUFFALO

The Brewster F2A Buffalo was originally intended to serve as a carrier-borne fighter for the United States Navy, but was not a success. Considerable numbers were acquired by the British and Netherlands Royal Air Forces for pilot training and as a stop-gap measure in Asia due to the demands for Spitfires and Hurricanes in other theatres. The Buffalo was not a match for the Japanese Navy's 'Zero' or the Imperial Army's Oscar, but performed reasonably well against the army Nakajima Ki-27 'Nate' fighter. Attempts to improve the Buffalo's performance by fitting lighter guns – Browning .30 calibre in place of the original .50 calibre – and carrying less fuel and ammunition came to nothing. Buffaloes were flown from stations in Singapore and Malaya by Australian, New Zealand and British squadrons.

several weaknesses: pilot protection was very poor; it was slow and prone to fuel problems at higher altitudes and to overheating. To make matters worse, when the Japanese struck nearly half of the fifty-two Buffaloes in the reserve stock were out of action through problems with a new engine design.

The rest of the combat aircraft consisted of a mixture of Blenheim bombers and twenty-four thoroughly obsolete Vickers Vildebeests. The situation was not helped by a general shortage of spare parts to keep the aircraft flying or by the lack of combat experience among the crews. Of the aircraft available, only the Blenheim was not outclassed by its Japanese counterparts, but without adequate fighter protection they would prove terribly vulnerable to the Zero and Oscar fighters of the enemy. Additionally, expectations were unrealistically high in the first days of the conflict. To an extent this was probably a legacy of the Battle of Britain in 1940, but there were two other factors: repeated claims that the Buffalo was more than a match for anything the Japanese had to offer, and that Japanese pilots were not particularly competent, not being able fly at night because of racially congenital eyesight problems. If the RAF was under-equipped in fighters and bombers, the situation was no better in regard to reconnaissance. Only three Catalina and seventeen Hudson aircraft were in service with another two Catalinas and seven Hudsons in reserve. RAF reconnaissance was effective at the beginning of the campaign, but although the approaching Japanese fleet was identified from the air by a Hudson on 6 December no action was taken by Far East Command.

British Ground Force

If Singapore was to be protected the airfields would need to be securely defended with thousands of men, but there would also need to be a powerful field army to repel an invasion by sea or overland from Thailand. Given the needs of the European and North African theatres, it was abundantly clear that troops would be increasingly hard to come by as the war progressed, but Percival was not actually short of troops; he was short of troops with sufficient training and he was short of adequate equipment.

Percival's immediate superior was General Archibald Wavell. The two men did not always see eye-to-eye on the general approach to the campaign, and Wavell's appreciation of the situation was not always very realistic. He did not know either the country or the troops and, initially, held the Japanese armed services in poor regard. Percival's relationship with his subordinates was not altogether positive either.

The chief assets of Malaya Command were III Indian Corps under Lieutenant General Sir Lewis Heath, 8th Australian Division under Major General Gordon Bennett; Singapore Fortress under Major General Keith Simmons; and 12th Indian Brigade under Brigadier Paris. Heath's position in the command structure was a difficult one. Unlike his colleagues – or his superior – he had recent senior battlefield experience as commander of 5th Indian Division in North Africa. He had very different views about the conduct of the campaign to Percival and suffered from his commander's

Sir Lewis Heath

Heath was born in 1885. He joined the Indian Army in 1906 and served until his retirement in 1946, save for the period between 1909 and 1913, when he served with the King's African Rifles. After the First World War he served in Persia and Afghanistan and was appointed to command 1st Battalion, 11th Sikh Regiment in 1930. He was an instructor on the staff of the Indian Army's Senior Officers' School at Belgaum from 1934–36.

At the outbreak of war in 1939 he was the commander of the 5th Indian Division based at Secunderabad. At that point the division consisted of two brigades, each of three battalions of Indian infantry. In 1940 5th Division was transferred to the Sudan, where it was joined by three British infantry battalions so that each brigade would have two Indian and one British battalion, which was the normal practice for Indian formations throughout the Second World War. The division served with some distinction in Eritrea in 1940, and in Egypt and Iraq in 1941, and it was from there that Heath – known widely as 'Piggy' – was appointed as commander of III Indian Corps in Malaya Command. Heath did not share his superior's views on the conduct of the campaign but was generally as supportive of Percival as he could be. He was taken prisoner in February 1942 and spent the next three and a half years in captivity in Taiwan and Manchuria.

7. Lt Gen. Sir Lewis Heath.

8. Indian mountain gunners in training.

general lack of respect for the Indian Army, of which General Heath was a product. His command covered the whole of northern Malaya and was, at best, an unwieldy structure. In addition to two divisions (9th and 11th Indian, though each had only two brigades instead of three) and the 28th Indian Independent Brigade, Heath had responsibility for Penang Fortress and three battalions assigned to airfield defence. Major General Barstow's 11th Division was stationed between Alor Setar and Sadao in the north-east, 40 miles away from divisional headquarters near Butterworth. The 9th Division was rather more scattered, with 8th Brigade at Kota Bahru and 22nd Brigade nearly 200 miles south at Kuantan. Although both brigades were on the east coast, divisional headquarters had been placed close to Heath's own HQ

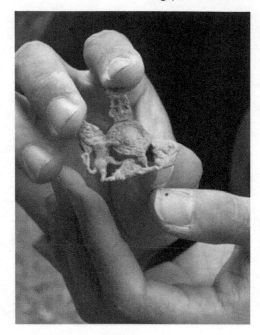

9. Battlefield Archaeology. A Cambridgeshire Regiment cap badge recovered by Glasgow University's Adam Park Project. (Jon Cooper)

in the vicinity of Kuala Lumpur, on the other side of the country. The remaining formation, 28th Indian, was at Ipoh, roughly equidistant from the other concentrations of the corps.

Bennett's 8th Australian Division, also of just two brigades, lay further to the south; 22nd Australian Brigade (Brigadier Taylor) was to the north of Mersing and 27th Australian Brigade (Brigadier Maxwell) near Kluang. Percival had distributed his forces widely to ensure that there were troops at all of the places most likely to be attacked, but in doing so had also ensured that none of his formations was in a position to move quickly to the support of any other.

If the general deployment was weak, contingency planning was no better. Arrangements had been made for a mobile force (to be known as *Krohcol*) to enter Thailand in the event of Japanese landings and to occupy a hillside road position known as 'the Ledge'. The plan was sound: blocking the Ledge

10. *Battlefield Archaeology. Glasgow University is conducting The Adam Park Project (TAPP) excavating an area where the Cambridgeshire Regiment was in action. (Jon Cooper)*

would undoubtedly stall the Japanese advance for a time and allow formations to be brought into the battle in a rational and effective manner, but there was no means of ensuring that the plan – Operation Matador – could be launched in time to secure the position. Additionally, little had been done to prepare for attack. Modest beach defences had been erected at various points, though many of them – notably those to the south of Kota Bahru – were only dummies.

Although III Corps was theoretically organised as a combat formation, in practice it was really more a loose collection of battalions scattered across the country. There had been very little in the way of brigade-level training, even less at divisional level and virtually none at corps level. Signals equipment was poor and in short supply, and the failure to conduct regular and challenging exercises meant that the signals staff had had no opportunity to develop techniques and practices. For the same reason, staff work was generally of a poor standard throughout the campaign, though there were some very creditable exceptions. There were plenty of excuses for these deficiencies – shortage of equipment and funds, the continual drain of key personnel to replace losses in the Middle East campaigns – but the single greatest barrier was that few people believed that the Japanese would attack and many of those who thought they might were far too confident that the enemy could be defeated quickly and easily. Shortages certainly were a real challenge, but, in all, Percival and Heath were responsible for doing everything they could to ensure that their troops were fit and ready for battle.

Inadequate training and preparation was not simply a question of failures at a senior level – though commanders should certainly have been making sure that the individual units were being properly prepared – but few of the infantry battalions were really in a condition to fight. Although there were several regular infantry battalions in Malaya Command, only one, 1st Argyll and Sutherland Highlanders, had been put through an appropriate training programme. The colonel, Ian Stewart, had adopted a rigorous regime as soon as his battalion arrived in Malaya from India early in 1941. As well as conducting regular exercises and rout marches to ensure fitness and proficiency, he had located some armoured cars in store in Singapore and had had them made ready for combat. Stewart's

11. *Argyll and Sutherland Highlanders in training.*

actions were seen as eccentric by many, but when the fighting started the Argylls proved to the most useful unit in the entire command. As Wavell put it:

> If all units in Malaya had been led with the same foresight and imagination that Brigadier Stewart showed with the training of his battalion, the story of the campaign might have been different. It was the realisation of this that led me to order Brigadier Stewart's return to India to impart his knowledge and ideas to units preparing for the return match with the Japanese.
>
> Major General Woodburn Kirby, *The War Against Japan*,
> HMSO, 1957

The price of being prepared for fighting in Malaya was that the Argylls would be called upon repeatedly to deal with crises and paid a heavy price in casualties, so much so that they would eventually have to have their numbers made up with Royal Marines from the *Repulse* and *Prince of Wales*, and would acquire the nickname 'Plymouth Argyles' on account of the name of the football team and the marines' long association with that town.

Commonwealth Troops

Although there were several British battalions, the majority of the infantry were either Indian or Australian. The Indian battalions came from two sources: either battalions of the Indian Army proper or units 'on loan' from independent Indian States Forces (ISF). When the war started in 1939 the Indian Army was subjected to a massive programme of expansion, which had been far too rapid to allow for proper training. Most of the officers were young British men, recently recruited and many not yet really competent in the languages of their soldiers. This was a major issue since, because of the very rapid expansion of the Indian Army, it had not been possible to ensure that units were composed of men from a single cultural background and it was not uncommon for two or three languages to be used in just one battalion.

In general, these newly raised units had not attained the high standards of the 4th and 5th Indian Divisions fighting in the desert or that would reach Burma, where by 1944 the majority of the infantry in the Fourteenth Army would be either Indian or African. By December 1941 some of the Indian battalions had been in Malaya for a long time, but few had been properly trained. Like the British battalions, this was, to some extent, a product of having to send trained officers, VCOs (Viceroy Commissioned Officers) and NCOs as replacements for the units in the Middle East, a process known as 'milking'. Some Indian officers had received only very rudimentary training before being posted to their units and some senior NCOs had been commissioned despite not really being suitable material.

VICEROY COMMISSIONED OFFICER

VCOs were officers in the Indian Army. They were junior in rank and status to king's commissioned officers, but superior to warrant officers. At the start of the war most commissioned officers in Indian regiments were British, though the proportion of Indian-born officers was rising steadily. Almost all VCOs were men with long records of exemplary service and provided a vital cultural and linguistic link to ensure an effective relationship between the officers and the ORs (other ranks). There were three grades of VCO in infantry battalions: jemadars, subedars and subedar-majors.

There were also acute shortages of particular items, notably mortars, light machine guns and Bren carriers. The infantry units were not alone in this. The officer shortage was made worse by the fact that many Indian officers of the pre-war regular army infantry units had been posted to newly raised artillery and armoured units training in India or North Africa. Tropical uniforms were available in adequate quantities, though the standard-issue British Army boots and thick socks can hardly have been comfortable. Almost all troops were issued with steel helmets, but considerable numbers wore general Service caps, regimental bonnets or old-fashioned 'solar topis'. British and Australian troops were issued with the same pattern of webbing as their comrades elsewhere and Indian troops with the similar 'India pattern' variant.

Many Indian Army units had no time to become acclimatised. For most of the men, Malaya was a very different environment from home and this was not always appreciated by British or Australian officers, some of whom rather assumed that all Asian populations grew up in much the same sort of climate. Some Indian units had almost no training at all. The men were recruited, put on ships and transported to Malaya on the assumption that there would be time to train them once they were 'in-country'. Overall, the remarkable thing is that so many Indian units performed as well as they did

Gordon Bennett

Born at Melbourne in 1887, Bennett served courageously and with distinction in the First World War. He fought at Gallipoli and in France, and acquired a CB, CMG and DSO, rising to the rank of brigadier at the age of 29. After the First World War he worked in textiles and as an accountant before becoming a senior local government official and the President of the Associated Chambers of Manufactures of Australia in 1933. He was appointed major general in the Australian Reserve forces in 1930. He was a fierce critic of Australian defence policy in general and published several articles attacking both the policies and the personnel of the Australian Army in 1937. Partly on account of those articles and partly because it was widely believed that he was not a suitable person to have a command that would involve co-operation with senior British officers, he was not appointed to a command in the Australian force in North Africa – he was just as critical of the British hierarchy as he was of his Australian superiors.

Constantly at odds with his colleagues, subordinates and superiors, Bennett was extremely critical of regular officers, but was appointed to command Australian 8th Division and posted to Singapore in February 1942. In this role he was adamant that his force should be kept intact rather than being split up to support other formations as needed. Unlike his superior, Percival, Bennett chose to abandon his post and escaped to Australia. Although he received a warm welcome from his political superiors, his actions were not appreciated in the Australian Army and by 1943 his career was effectively over; by mid-1944 he had been moved on to the reserve list. He published a book, *Why Singapore Fell*, which was highly critical of all of his colleagues.

12. *Lt Gen. Percival and Maj. Gen. Bennett.*

in the Malayan campaign, and it is hardly surprising that many thousands chose to join the India National Army (INA).

The Malay Regiment and the various local volunteer units were, naturally, better used to the climate, but they were few in number and, like the rest of Malaya Command, were bedevilled by shortages or obsolescent equipment. Local recruitment did not extend to the large Chinese population until the very end of the campaign, when the battle was already lost.

Pre-war Australia had several reserve forces divisions that were expanded rapidly on the outbreak of war in 1939. Few of the officers, even at brigade and battalion commander level, were professional soldiers. Most 8th Division troops volunteered after the fall of France in June 1940 and had, therefore, been in uniform for more than a year at the beginning of the Malayan campaign.

The Australian policy of giving troops their basic training at home, rather than continuing the process once they arrived overseas, meant that the troops were trained for and in the location to which they were posted. In general this was a sensible policy since it did lead to good standards overall, but it meant that replacements joining the division in the later stages of the battle had not been either fully trained or acclimatised. An infantry division is designed to act as a team, and 8th Division never received its third brigade. Furthermore, though there was a policy that Australian forces should always act as clearly defined entities, operational requirements and questionable policies forced the two brigades to operate separately, thus arguably compromising organisation in battle. There had been relatively little brigade- or divisional-level training to integrate the units properly, so it is unclear how much difference dividing the formation really made once the campaign was underway, but it clearly did not help. Equally, there had been no serious corps-level training at all with the formations of Malaya Command, so none of the divisional or brigade headquarters were fully competent to run battles.

The situation was not helped by the divisional commander, Gordon Bennett. Bennett had served in the First World War, commanding a battalion and later a brigade with some skill, and had served as commander of a militia division before the war. His success in the Great War perhaps helped to encourage his total confidence in his own abilities in 1941–42.

His lack of belief in his fellow commanders – though not entirely misplaced – undermined confidence in Percival and Heath throughout Malaya Command. Abrasive and over-confident, he managed to alienate most of his brigade and battalion commanders, especially the regulars, since he was strongly prejudiced in favour of reserve officers like himself. Bennett held strong views about the nature of operations required, but was not adept at ensuring they were actually mounted. He had no confidence in Percival at all and was willing to go behind his commander's back or over his head to avoid doing anything he did not want to do.

Organisation

Infantry units throughout the British Empire and Commonwealth conformed to a common organisation. Each battalion had four rifle companies divided into four platoons and each platoon into three 'sections' of ten men. The standard firearm of all the Allied infantry, British, Indian and Australian, was the Lee-Enfield .303 calibre rifle. A reliable and accurate bolt-action weapon with a ten-round magazine, the Lee-Enfield was far superior to the Japanese Arisaka. In addition to the Lee-Enfields, each section had a Bren light machine gun. The Bren – like the Lee-Enfield – was a fine piece of equipment. The magazine could take thirty rounds, though it was common practice to load with only twenty-eight to reduce strain on the magazine spring and prevent jamming. Experience in France in 1940 had shown the need for another automatic weapon at section level. The Sten gun had been invented to fill this need along with large purchases of Thompson sub-machine guns from the United States, but many units in Malaya Command did not receive either in adequate quantities due to the demands of other theatres.

VICKERS

The Vickers gun was adopted by the British Army in 1912 and became the standard machine gun for all the Commonwealth countries. It was gas operated and the barrel was cooled by a water-filled jacket. Despite the tropical heat, the Vickers gun performed admirably in Malaya and Singapore. The gun fired the same .303 calibre bullets as the Lee-Enfield rifle and the Bren gun, but from 250-round canvas belts. Each battalion had a machine-gun platoon usually with four weapons and with six to eight men per gun; two to operate the weapon and the others to carry ammunition and provide protection for the gun team.

13. The Vickers machine gun was the standard for all Commonwealth countries. This one in use in Malaya, December 1941.

In theory, each infantry battalion also had a machine-gun platoon with Vickers .303in machine guns and a mortar platoon with 3in mortars. These were both good-quality weapons, but again the demands of other theatres had taken precedence and several battalions did not have their full complement. The battalion-level anti-tank weapon was the Boyes anti-tank rifle, a 0.5in bolt-action weapon, which was completely obsolete in Europe and North Africa against German and Italian vehicles, but could still make an impression on some of the lighter Japanese armoured cars and tanks.

One of the peculiarities of the British approach to combat was the Bren carrier. This lightly armoured tracked vehicle was put to innumerable uses, but its chief function was to provide rapid intervention and support for the rifle companies. Although a good deal of the tactical practice of an infantry battalion revolved around its carrier platoon, many units in Malaya Command did not have their full complement and some had none at all.

A great weakness in Malaya Command was communication. There was little wireless equipment and a good deal of what was available was not very effective. Laying cables for field telephones

14. A Bren light machine gun on a tripod mount; a rare configuration. (Joost J. Bakker)

BREN CARRIERS

More Bren carriers were produced than any other armoured vehicle in history. Initially issued in small numbers to infantry battalions as transport for heavy equipment such as mortars, by late 1941 every battalion was supposed to have a 'carrier platoon' with 2in mortars and Bren guns to provide rapid support as required. Few of the infantry battalions in Malaya Command had their full complement of carriers and some none at all.

was slow and cumbersome and the cables themselves were very vulnerable to artillery fire.

Artillery

The artillery element of Malaya Command suffered from the same problems as the infantry. Most of the field artillery regiments had been issued with the excellent 25-pounder gun/howitzer, but because of the demands of the North Africa campaign several units had only two batteries of eight guns rather than three. The anti-tank regiments were, in the main, at full strength with forty-eight 2-pounder guns each. The 2-pounder was reasonably accurate and had a good rate of fire, but was relatively slow to deploy. Like the Boyes rifle, it had been made obsolete by the rapid development of armour in European armies, but it was capable of holding its own against Japanese tanks and armoured cars.

The most significant weakness on the ground lay in the complete absence of tanks. British tanks were not particularly well armoured or well armed, though many models were mechanically reliable. The various Vickers light tanks and the Matilda and Valentine models had proved to be entirely inadequate against the Axis forces in the desert, where a high degree of visibility often meant a British vehicle could be knocked out of action long before it was close enough to engage effectively, but these same vehicles

15. Japanese anti-tank rifle. Developed in the First World War, anti-tank rifles were largely obsolete before 1941, but were capable of penetrating the light armour of the few Allied armoured cars in Malaya. (Author's collection)

16. Battlefield Archaeology. An example of the Japanese anti-tank rifle. The tropical climate means that most material degrades very quickly. (Author's collection)

would have been on a par with their Japanese counterparts. The lack of tanks was not caused by demands elsewhere, but had been a matter of policy. Although General Bond had asked for at least one regiment of medium tanks as early as 1940, there was a near-universal assumption that tanks could not operate in the terrain of Malaya.

17. 25-pounder field guns at Sentosa, Singapore. (Author's collection)

25-POUNDER GUN

The 25-pounder was the standard field artillery piece of the Royal Artillery and with Commonwealth armies throughout the Second World War; it remained in service until the 1960s and well beyond in other countries. Each field regiment was equipped with twenty-four guns divided into three batteries of eight, each comprising two troops of four and they in turn consisted of two sections of two guns each. Strictly speaking, the 25-pounder was a 'gun/howitzer' since it could fire in both the lower register (0–45 degrees) and the upper register (45–90 degrees). The gun provided sterling service in Malaya despite the hot and damp conditions, though several regiments had only two batteries instead of three.

2-POUNDER AT GUN

The 2-pounder was the standard British and Commonwealth anti-tank gun at the beginning of the Second World War. Although it was originally designed to be mounted in tank turrets, the army sought a surface mounting so that it could be used by anti-tank regiments or anti-tank platoons in infantry battalions. The carriage adopted had three legs, two of which folded up under the gun whilst in transport. Those two legs and the wheels had to be moved to position the gun for action, which made it difficult to deploy quickly, but once it was ready the gun could traverse easily through 360 degrees. By late 1941 the 2-pounder had been outclassed by German and Italian tanks but it was quite capable of penetrating the relatively thin and poor-quality hulls of the Japanese Chi-Ha and Ha-Go.

There was a modest supply of armoured cars, mostly Marmon-Herringtons and Lanchesters, but these were slow and lightly armoured. None of them mounted anything heavier than a machine gun and were therefore clearly incapable of standing up to Japanese tanks. The problems were multiplied by an almost total deficiency in training. The Indian 3rd Cavalry had their horses replaced with armoured cars but had had virtually no training at all, with the result that almost all of their vehicles were written off before they could go into action. In addition, because of the assumption that Malaya was not suitable territory for armoured conflict, none of the infantry units had had any worthwhile training in dealing with armoured attacks; many soldiers had never even seen a tank before they encountered them on the battlefield.

The assumptions about the 'impenetrable jungle' and the impracticality of armoured warfare were simply ridiculous and should have been challenged by the senior officers in Malaya Command. Armies in general – and tanks in particular – travel along roads primarily, only deploying to countryside when

18. Rubber plantation. The endless rows of trees had a depressing effect on many troops. (Author's collection)

LANCHESTER ARMOURED CAR

The first Lanchester armoured cars entered service with the British Army in 1929. Lanchesters had a nominal top speed of about 50mph and a range of about 250 miles. They were armed with two .303 Vickers guns and one 0.5 calibre Vickers. In North Africa, Lanchesters proved to be obsolete and a considerable number were sent to India and the Far East. The story goes that Colonel Ian Stewart of the Argyll and Sutherland Highlanders found that there were some in store on Singapore and promptly 'acquired' them and put them to use in exercises with his battalion.

obstructed by the enemy, and although there were few roads running east–west across the country, there were fine highways running south from Thailand to Singapore. Tactical assumptions made once the campaign started were often just as bad. Wavell's instructions to Percival that he should fight the 'main battle' in areas where his 'superior artillery' could be used to advantage were not superficially unreasonable, but rather depended on the belief that the Japanese artillery was not capable of effective counter-battery work. In practice, poor communications, poor training, a failure to ensure adequate supplies of ammunition and the inability to stem Japanese advance undermined the premise. After the lengthy retreat down the peninsula, the troops were not confident in combat and became increasingly unlikely to make a determined stand. Often, when they did stop the Japanese advance, they were obliged to retire because of threats to their flanks or breakthroughs against other units that might result in encirclement. A number of withdrawals occurred due to misleading orders or to the perceived need to maintain the integrity of formations as viable combat assets.

CHI-HA TANK

Designated the Type 97 from the Imperial year of 2597. The original main armament was a low-velocity 57mm gun, later exchanged for a high-velocity 47mm gun with better armour-piercing capability. The Chi-Ha was also equipped with two 7.7mm machine guns, one on the hull of the vehicle, the other mounted facing backwards from the turret – a very unusual arrangement. The turret armour was 25mm (1in) thick on the turret, which made the Chi-Ha very vulnerable to even light anti-tank weapons. The 21.7L diesel engine gave the 15-ton Chi-Ha a top speed of 24mph and a range of about 160 miles. Over 1,000 Chi-Ha tanks were built and they saw service in Malaya with 1st, 6th and 14th Tank Regiments.

19. A speeding Ha-Go Type 95 tank.

HA-GO TANK

Production of the Type 95 Ha-Go, also known as the Kyu-Go, was the most common Japanese tank of the Second World War, with over 2,300 vehicles produced between 1935 and 1943, including a field engineering crane and an amphibious version. Ha-Go tanks were at least as good as any light tank in the world when they were introduced in 1935, and were a match for the Honey (or Stuart) tanks they encountered in Burma and the Pacific in terms of speed and manoeuvrability. The Ha-Go was driven by a 14L Mitsubishi diesel engine and armed with a 37mm gun and two 7.7mm machine guns. Some hundreds of Ha-Go tanks were captured by Chinese forces at the end of the Second World War and they saw extensive service in the Chinese Civil War between the Nationalists and the Communists.

Misconceptions & Shortcomings

In addition to the problems with shortages, poor equipment and inadequate training, the Allied commanders underestimated the Japanese to a ridiculous degree. To some extent this was simply racism. The notion that the Japanese were short, were poor physical specimens generally, had poor eyesight and that their equipment was bad was compounded by faulty strategic and tactical analysis. Japan had already been at war for some years and gained a wealth of experience, but Westerners did not see Chinese forces as serious opposition. The fact that Japan had been roundly defeated by the Soviet Union in 1938 and that now – at the end of 1941 – the Russians were being heavily beaten by the Germans did not mean that the Japanese were incompetent, but that was the general perception of the British military establishment.

None of this was helped by a policy position at Westminster that can only be described as wishful thinking. The assumption that there would not be war in the East ignored the possibility that Japan might see the European war as an opportunity.

By the time General Yamashita's troops reached Johore, very little of any value had been done to prepare Singapore for a siege. Claims that Singapore was an 'impregnable fortress' bore no relation to reality. There were a number of defensive installations dating from the construction of the Singapore naval base. A dozen batteries had been erected and equipped with 6in or 9.2in guns, but they had all been located on the southern coast of the island, on the assumption that any threat to Singapore would come from the sea, not overland from Malaya. By good fortune it transpired that most of the guns would be able to fire to the north, but there was a severe shortage of suitable ammunition. The majority of the supply available consisted of armour-piercing shells that would be effective against ships; there was very few of the high-explosive shells required to break up attacks on land.

20. Pre-war concrete emplacement for a 9.2in gun. (Author's collection)

In the last weeks of the campaign on the mainland some effort was made to provide defences on the northern shore, but little progress was made. It was difficult to procure labour since the civil authorities would not allow Percival to pay an adequate wage. An attempt was made to keep the preparations secret from the community for fear that there would be a decline in morale, though it was obviously impractical to maintain security with so many people working on defences. Such work as was undertaken was increasingly at risk from Japanese air attacks. When the bombers came into view, the labourers would scatter and it was very difficult to persuade them to go back to work if there was not going to be any friendly air cover. A number of concrete machine-gun positions had been built in the 1930s and a few more once the campaign started, but they were few in number and far too widely scattered.

Much more could have been done to protect the island; mines and barbed wire were available in the sense that there were extensive stocks of both, but poor record keeping meant that no one knew where they were stored and a general lack of urgency meant that no one tried very hard to find them. In the final days before the battle there was a little more urgency, but some of the arrangements and propositions smacked of fantasy. There were not enough searchlights to cover all the likely landing areas and there were plans to use car headlights. Providing power for headlights other than by leaving them mounted on cars with the engines running would obviously be a challenge, but the illumination would have been marginal anyway.

The civil defence arrangements were equally poor. During the first air raid on the city all the lights were left on because no-one knew how to switch them off, aircraft were not scrambled for fear of friendly fire and there was a general lack of night-fighter training. There was very little in the way of an Air Raid Precautions (ARP) system and very few shelters. The latter was, admittedly, something of a challenge given the very low water table: the floors of even relatively shallow slit trenches tended to become a soggy quagmire in no time at all.

The appointment of a resident minister to ensure all was being done that could be done did not help. Sir Alfred 'Duff' Cooper arrived in 1941 but found he was obstructed at every turn by the governor, Sir Shenton Thomas. Cooper probably did not have the relevant skills or experience to make a great impression on the situation, and he certainly did not have the powers to do so. Although he did manage to secure the appointment of one person to co-ordinate all civil defence efforts in Singapore and Johore, Shenton Thomas ensured that the appointee – Brigadier Simpson – was denied the powers to do the job. Other than a desire to preserve his own authority as governor in all matters, it is impossible to see why Thomas should have been so obstructive; however, he did not get on well with Cooper and may have acted out of nothing more than resentment.

The Japanese Army

The general ethos of the Japanese Army could hardly have been more different to those of Britain, India or Australia. Encouraged to be self-reliant and treated with ruthless brutality, the Japanese soldiers' training instilled confidence in battle and a high degree of physical fitness. Prior to the invasion, only one regiment had engaged in any degree of jungle training, so the average Japanese soldier was no more familiar with the combat environment than his British or Indian counterpart; the difference was that he had been taught not to fear the jungle, whereas most Allied troops had been conditioned to avoid it.

Japanese Army staff work and the ability to improvise had been honed by years of fighting in China, where considerable distances and a poor transport infrastructure posed major problems with supplies. The term 'army' as in 'Twenty-Fifth Army' really equates to the term 'corps' in other armies. An 'army' was not so much a permanent administrative structure as a group of divisions brought together for a particular campaign. The Twenty-Fifth Army consisted of the three infantry divisions, 5th, 18th and the

21. *Waxwork effigy of a Japanese soldier with an Arisaka rifle at the Siloso Fort Museum, Singapore.*

Imperial Guards, supported by elements of four medium and light tank regiments.

The Japanese divisional structure varied considerably throughout the war and from one theatre to another, but 5th and 18th Divisions in 1941 each had two infantry brigades, each of two regiments comprising three battalions; some twelve infantry battalions in total. Each division had an artillery regiment, a reconnaissance unit and various divisional troops. The Imperial Guards Division and 5th Division were entirely motorised, but 18th Division's transport was horse drawn and the reconnaissance unit was a cavalry battalion. The division started the campaign with nearly 6,000 horses, which may seem anachronistic, but in fact almost all of the German divisions other than those in North Africa had horse-drawn transport and artillery throughout the Second World War. The Guards Division had nine battalions in three regiments and although the formation enjoyed a certain status, it was, arguably, the least effective of the three divisions in the Twenty-Fifth Army.

With about thirty officers and a little over 1,000 men at full strength, the Japanese infantry battalion was rather larger than its Commonwealth counterpart and consisted of a headquarters company, a machine-gun company and four rifle companies. The companies, again bigger than their Commonwealth equivalent, had a headquarters company, three rifle platoons each with three squads of thirteen men commanded by a corporal or sergeant, and a grenade discharger squad of thirteen men to give a total company roll of about 200. The standard rifle was the Type 99 Arisaka, a bolt action weapon of 7.7mm calibre; however, some of the earlier Type 38 models (6.5mm calibre) were still in use, which complicated ammunition supply. The Japanese infantrymen had a rather ramshackle appearance which belied their fighting ability. Their cotton uniforms came in a wide variety of shades of khaki, green and grey, and the puttees worn by many gave them a somewhat old-fashioned look. Steel helmets were issued as standard, but some chose to wear 'solar topi'-type sun helmets.

22. Japanese machine-gun crew.

Soft rubber-soled shoes were popular and gave the advantage of virtual silence on the battlefield, but most soldiers wore slightly curious footwear with a separation to accommodate the big toe.

The standard squad light machine gun was the dependable and accurate Type 99, which was very similar in appearance to the British Bren gun, even to the thirty-round curved magazine. Japanese officers were expected to purchase their own pistols and many favoured foreign-made weapons over the underpowered and unreliable Nambu models. Japanese officers and NCOs were much more inclined to carry swords into battle. Some were treasured antiques handed down through generations; others were mass-produced weapons of poor quality. One squad in each platoon was equipped with the Type 89 grenade discharger, which could fire a fragmentation grenade or a high-explosive shell weighing about 2lb. The platoon's offensive power went some way to compensate for the lack of a mortar platoon at battalion level, as was common practice in most armies.

Each regiment had an integral gun company with two sections, each with two 75mm guns, and an anti-tank gun

ARISAKA

The Arisaka was the standard rifle of the Imperial Japanese Army throughout the war, though in practice a large number of its predecessor, the Type 38, remained in use because Japanese industry could not meet the demands of the army. The Arisaka took a 7.7mm cartridge and had a five-round box magazine. Introduced in 1939, the Arisaka was, overall, a good-quality weapon, though neither as sturdy nor as accurate as the Allied Lee-Enfield and with only half the magazine capacity; the quality of production also declined after 1942. Over 3 million Arisakas were made; many saw service with Indonesian nationalists after the war.

23. *Riflemen with the Arisaka rifle.*

JAPANESE PISTOLS

The Japanese Army adopted only one revolver, the model 26. It was a double-action, 9mm, six-shot weapon based largely on Smith and Wesson designs of the late nineteenth century. The most common automatic pistol was the Type 14 Nambu, which fired a low-velocity 8mm round. Neither model was especially popular and, since Japanese officers were obliged to provide their own side arms, many of them chose to purchase foreign models privately or to acquire them on the battlefield. The Nambu was quite accurate, but was prone to jamming. Something in the region of 200,000 Nambus were produced between 1906 and the end of the war in 1945.

company of six 37mm or 47mm guns. Each division would normally have one regiment of field artillery, one of engineers, a transport regiment, a signals unit and a medical unit; however, divisional structure varied widely depending on location and the nature of the formation. A division with horse transport required a lot more manpower so, for example, with strength of 22,000 men, 18th Division was almost half as large again as 5th Division with 15,000.

A divisional field artillery regiment would usually have one howitzer and two field-gun batteries. The gun battalions consisted of three batteries each with three sections of two 75mm pieces, a total of eighteen guns. The howitzer regiment would normally have four batteries each with two sections of two 105mm weapons, a total of sixteen.

Estimates of the number of tanks available to the Twenty-Fifth Army run as high as a little over 300. The British Official History gives figures of 70 medium and 100 light tanks but makes no mention of armoured cars at all, though some were certainly in use with reconnaissance units. The Japanese never really developed an armoured doctrine as such and the normal practice was to deploy tanks as infantry support. Since they encountered

KNEE MORTARS

The Type 89 Grenade Discharger was widely known as the 'knee mortar' by Allied troops throughout the Asia and Pacific theatres, from the widely held belief that the weapon could be fired when braced against the thigh; a practice which would almost certainly result in a broken femur or hip. The discharger was issued in large quantities – often fifty or more to a battalion – and was in service from 1929 until the end of the war. Smoke, incendiary, fragmentation and high-explosive rounds were available and large numbers were used by the Indonesian forces during the war of independence against the Netherlands from 1945.

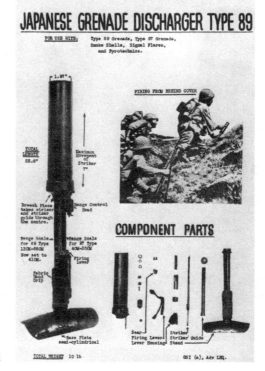

24. The Japanese knee mortar grenade launcher.

very little in the way of enemy tanks in China and none at all in Malaya, Japanese armoured units enjoyed great success and carried out some daring and devastating forays penetrating positions, seizing bridges before they could be demolished and overrunning columns of Allied transport or artillery units that were still limbered up. Bicycles – either army issue or seized from civilians – were used in great number and to great effect. As tyres wore out, they were discarded and the troops cycled on the bare rims of the wheels. On at least one occasion the grinding, rattling mechanical noise generated was mistaken by Allied troops for tanks.

The Japanese military establishment did not include a separate air service, but two bodies: the army air force and the

25. Making gas masks in Singapore.

navy air force. In late 1941 the two air arms had well over 4,000 combat aircraft, but low industrial capacity meant that losses could not be made good – a problem that was exacerbated by the increasing difficulty of getting materials to the factories because of attacks on Japanese shipping and bombing raids on the factories themselves.

In Malaya the Twenty-Fifth Army was supported by 3rd (Army) Air Division. Air divisions nominally consisted of two or three 'Air Brigades'. Each brigade would generally consist of either three of four 'Air Regiments' and often with more than one type of aircraft in each regiment. The regiment would normally have three squadrons of either nine bombers or sixteen fighters so one regiment might

HURRICANE FIGHTER

Designed by Sydney Camm and brought into service in 1937, the Hurricane was the workhorse fighter of the Royal Air Force. Over 14,000 Hurricanes were built – 10 per cent of them in Canada – before production ceased in 1944. The Hurricane was a big improvement on the Buffalo fighters which had been deployed to Malaya and Singapore, but struggled against the Japanese 'Nate' and 'Zero' fighters. The Hurricane was normally equipped with four 20mm cannon, had a maximum speed of 340mph and a range of 600 miles.

26. Hawker Hurricane Mk IIC. (Ad Meskens)

ZERO FIGHTER

The official Allied code name for the Mitsubishi A6M Zero was 'Zeke', though the name is seldom used. The Zero was built for the Imperial Japanese Navy as a carrier-borne fighter and entered service in 1940. For the first two years of the war the Zero enjoyed great success in combat, being more than a match for the Buffalo and Hurricane fighters deployed against them in Malaya. Although the Zero was not as fast as the Spitfire or the Hurricane, she was more manoeuvrable and had a better rate of climb. The Zero weighed about 2½ tons when fully fuelled and armed, carrying two 7.7mm machine guns, two 20mm cannon and two 60kg bombs. As the war progressed, naval fighter development failed to match that of the Allies. Over 10,000 Zero fighters were built between 1940 and 1945.

27. A long-wrecked Japanese Zero fighter plane of the Second World War. (Bartosz Cieslak)

have anywhere between twenty-seven and forty-eight combat aircraft in total. Airfields were staffed by specialist battalions with responsibility for the defence and maintenance of the airfield and the provision of ordnance for regiments on their station, while the air regiment staff tended the aircraft.

The most well known of the Japanese aircraft of the Second World War is the A6M Zero, a carrier-borne fighter. The Imperial Army's Nate and Oscar fighters were probably a more familiar sight over the skies of Malaya and Singapore. The Nate was somewhat dated by 1941 but was still widely used as a bomber escort, but the Oscar was a first-rate aircraft more than capable of taking on the Brewster Buffaloes (the only Allied fighters in the theatre at the beginning of the campaign) and were a match for the Hurricanes, which arrived in the closing stages of the fighting. The Zero was completely underestimated by the British, despite the fact that they had been given all of the information relating to the aircraft by Chinese government sources after a Zero had been captured intact.

Perhaps the single most telling strike by air power in the whole conflict was the destruction of the *Prince of Wales* and the *Repulse* (Force Z) as they steamed toward Kuantan with the intention of disrupting reported Japanese landings there. Force Z was struck on the morning of 10 December 1941 by a succession of 'Nell' torpedo bombers operating from airfields in French Indo-China. Sinking the two ships was not simply a blow to the power of the navy; it was a great blow to both civilian and military morale and rather set the tone for the rest of the campaign. Of all the navies in the world, the British should have been more aware of the power of aircraft at sea since just the year before a force of obsolete Fairey Swordfish torpedo bombers had destroyed one Italian battleship and severely damaged another two in an attack on Taranto.

The Type 99 'Sally', Type 99 'Lily' and Mitsubishi G4M 'Betty' bombers, among others, were used extensively throughout the Malayan campaign. Due to poor surface-to-air communications, the army air service provided little in the way of integrated air support for troops on the ground and much of its effort was focused on bombing towns and cities. The scarcity of anti-aircraft guns and limited quantities of ammunition, coupled with the sheer overwhelming numbers of Japanese aircraft, meant that there was little the Allies could do to prevent them from attacking. Although considerable damage was done to harbour facilities in Singapore, the chief purpose of the raids was to disrupt communications and demoralise the military and civilian population, a process which became more and more successful as it became apparent that the Allies could do nothing to prevent the attacks.

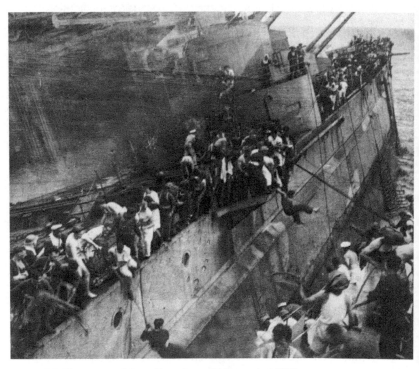

28. The rescue of Force Z survivors, 10 December 1941.

'BETTY'

With a top speed of about 250mph and a weapon payload of over ¾ ton, the 'Betty' – or Mitsubishi G4M – was comparable to other twin-engined bombers of her class, but was very vulnerable. To keep overall weight down – and consequently achieve a better speed – there was virtually no protection for the crew and the lack of self-sealing fuel tanks made the 'Betty' very vulnerable in combat. A number of 'Bettys' were used in the torpedo-bomber role against the *Prince of Wales* and the *Repulse*.

29. *An Imperial Japanese Navy Mitsubishi G4M 'Betty' bomber.*

THE DAYS
BEFORE BATTLE

Percival's general policy was unsuitable and unworkable in the circumstances of late 1941, and was not especially consistent. His initial troop commitments were not particularly rational and became increasingly irrelevant as the campaign developed. The prize – at least in the British view – was the great Singapore naval base, which could only be protected if there was adequate air power available, and the air power could only be maintained and adequately deployed if there were enough airfields to support the aircraft, but defending the airfields meant a heavy commitment of army resources. The necessary aircraft were not available, so protection of the fields was, essentially, redundant from the very beginning of the campaign. In addition to airfield protection, Percival also had to find the means of repelling an invasion wherever a force might land.

Percival did not develop a consistent policy for the campaign, but also failed to adjust his thinking to the situation, often endeavouring to make the circumstances fit the plan rather than the other way around. He alternated between plans to develop a strong defensive line, which would force the Japanese to concentrate their forces where his own troops would be able to take advantage of the superior British artillery, and a policy of slowing the Japanese advance while preparing for what he called 'the main battle' further south. Neither policy was really valid since neither gave any real consideration to what the enemy intended to do or how he intended to achieve his aims. Some of the 'wishful thinking' among the British command generally – not just Percival – was the product of unrealistic assessments of both the Allied and Japanese capabilities – the belief that the Japanese advance could be stopped in its tracks by artillery being a case in point. The British and Commonwealth forces did have a considerable quantity of high-quality artillery, but had not developed the necessary integration within divisional structures to make it effective.

Equally, the policy of a gradual withdrawal while preparing for a 'main battle' would have been a challenge for a highly trained and well-articulated army with confidence in itself and its leaders. There was nothing intrinsically wrong with the troops of Malaya Command, but it was not a trained and cohesive force. Poor leadership, bad decisions and unworkable policies, combined with a complete absence of armour, inefficient communications and totally inadequate air cover made Malaya Command formations extremely vulnerable to the daring and well-coordinated manoeuvres of the Japanese Army.

Whether the campaign would be a matter of forcing the Japanese to attack a strong defensive line and bring about static warfare, or of forcing them to take heavy casualties en route to a concentrated battle in southern Malaya was really not a decision that Percival could make; General Yamashita would not allow him that luxury. His policy was based on what Japanese commanders called a 'driving charge'. His troops were to force battle on the enemy at every opportunity and to pursue him relentlessly, specifically to prevent him regrouping either to build a defensive line or concentrate for a major battle.

In order to achieve and maintain the tempo necessary for such a policy, Yamashita's army needed to focus their attack along the excellent road system. This was not lost on British commanders, who tried repeatedly to deny passage to enemy forces. These

Tomoyuki Yamashita

Born in 1885 in the Kochi prefecture, Shikoku, Tomoyuki Yamashita joined the army in 1905 and first saw active service against the Germans in Shantung, China, in 1914. He graduated from the Imperial Army War College in 1916 and was a military attaché at Berne from 1919–22. He was an advocate of a political movement known as the 'Imperial way', which put him at odds with several of his contemporaries and superiors. Yamashita served as Japan's military attaché in Vienna, Austria, in 1928, but had retired to Japan to command an infantry regiment by the end of 1930. His view that Japan should extricate herself from the war in China and avoid war with Britain and the United States made him unpopular, and for some time he was relegated to a backwater post in the Kwantung Army.

He was appointed to the command of the Twenty-Fifth Army only a month before the invasion and became known as the 'Tiger of Malaya' on account of his remarkable success. He fell out of favour again in 1942 for referring to the people of Singapore as 'citizens of the Empire of Japan', which was contrary to the general policy that people in occupied territories should be subjects with duties and obligations, not citizens with rights. Yamashita spent the next two years in Manchuria, far from the main theatres of the war. Recalled to service in 1944, Yamashita fought with skill and tenacity. His attempt to prevent Manila from becoming a battlefield by withdrawing all Japanese forces without a fight was foiled by Admiral Iwabuchi, who seized the city with a large force of Imperial Navy infantry and military police units.

After a very questionable trial in which the prosecution accepted hearsay evidence and anonymous witnesses, Yamashita was sentenced to death and hanged. What are claimed to be the steps to the scaffold are preserved in the Penang War Museum.

30. Yamashita and Percival discussing surrender, 15 February 1942.

attempts were sometimes relatively successful in the short term, but were never really effective. In part this was due to the Japanese superiority in armour. The Allied anti-tank weapons were not ineffective, but they lacked the mobility of tanks. When the Japanese encountered serious resistance they simply moved infantry off the road and searched for flanks of the defenders. Once they had located the limits of the Allied deployment, they 'hooked' back on to the road behind the defenders and encircled them, preventing communications and reinforcements, or at least forcing a withdrawal. This quickly led to a culture of retreat. At a tactical level, battalion and brigade commanders were reluctant to risk the destruction of their command in actions that were, ostensibly, peripheral to the 'main battle' planned for the near future; in fact, they were repeatedly advised not to risk heavy casualties. At a more personal level it bred a degree of reluctance among the troops. If the Japanese could not be stopped, why should a soldier risk his life if his unit was going to be withdrawn in the near future anyway?

Within a matter of days, the pattern for the whole campaign had been set – the Japanese pushed forward as quickly as they could and the Allied commanders tried to maintain the integrity of their formations as they retreated. To some extent this was not unwise; if there was to be a 'main battle' in southern Malaya, the army had to be preserved as an effective force. The two problems being that the army as a whole was not an effective force in the first place and that the failure to impose much in the way of delay on the Japanese meant that the formations could not be properly rested, replenished and re-equipped to take a useful role as the campaign progressed.

Inadequate communications, incompetent staff work and a rapidly developing disposition toward retreat made the situation worse than it needed to be. On the occasions where Allied troops inflicted a local defeat on the Japanese they were often withdrawn because they were in danger of becoming isolated, but sometimes they were pulled out of action through sheer incompetence.

On a number of occasions, the Japanese were able to make an advance simply because there was nobody to delay them. On others, they were able to make breakthroughs that took them well into the Allied lines of communication and to destroy or capture great quantities of men and materiel, simply because there were no supporting Allied troops in place when a front-line unit was overrun or forced to abandon the road and take cover in the countryside. Naturally, news of such incidents travelled quickly among other units in the area and lost nothing in the telling, thus encouraging the belief that the Allied forces were incapable of standing up to the Japanese. Given the huge propaganda effort that had gone into convincing Allied troops in general – and British troops in particular – that the Japanese were racially inferior and that their equipment was poor, it is hardly surprising that Malaya Command as a whole was in something of a state of shock well before the end of January 1942. The morale of the troops had been badly undermined by constant retreating and the fact that the skies were dominated by the Japanese, as well as the loss of the only two major warships in the theatre.

Things were no better at the top of the command structure. Wavell was not really in tune with the battle at any point and was unable to instil a sense of purpose in Percival and also did not have the authority to force Shenton Thomas to make any kind of positive contribution to the war effort, which helped to undermine Percival's authority and confidence. Percival's policy was to inflict as much damage as possible during a slow retreat, but he was not prepared to make units fight to the last while others withdrew to more favourable positions. General Heath had always favoured a general withdrawal so that the Japanese could be engaged from a position of greater strength in northern Johore, rather than wearing the troops out with continual actions that seemed to do little or nothing to impede the Japanese advance. General Bennett was utterly dismissive of all soldiers except the Australians and cheerfully undermined all of his colleagues and most of his subordinates.

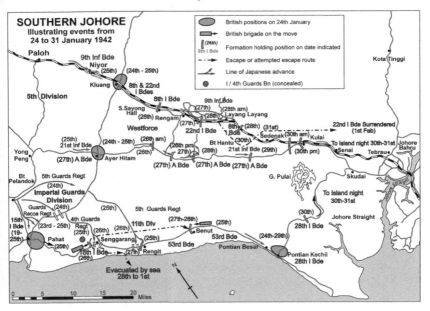

Withdrawal to Singapore, 24–31 January 1942.

The plan to engage the Japanese in a 'main battle' in Johore gained general acceptance among the commanders; the problem lay in the fact that the Japanese advance was too rapid to allow the Allies to concentrate their forces. Air superiority made movement by day dangerous and poor communications made movement by night very difficult. In fact, the Japanese were not able to make the best use of their air power because their ground forces had very little communication with the air arm. Once the RAF had been defeated, Japanese pilots were mostly limited to seeking targets of opportunity. With better integration between aircraft and troops the campaign would have been even shorter. With precious few aircraft at all, the Allies were unable to make any impression on the fragile Japanese lines of communication. A small number of modest raids were staged from the sea, but little was achieved.

The main battle in Johore never really materialised and the Allies staged a withdrawal to Singapore in the last days of January 1942. Percival believed that the island could withstand a siege – it was, after all, described as a 'fortress'. The term was, however, misleading. In British military parlance 'fortress' was an administrative term used to describe an area with a large concentration of troops. It did not imply that there were extensive fortifications, but understandably this was a distinction that meant nothing to almost everybody concerned.

The coastal batteries had not been designed to provide fire plans to deter a crossing of the Johore Strait and the defensive positions on the northern shore were too far apart to support one another or to provide a continuous line of strongholds. The installations were vulnerable to isolation and to a great extent the Japanese knew where they were. Throughout the 1920s and 1930s Japan had mounted a major intelligence operation in Singapore. Agents working as bar girls, photographers, barbers and in a host of other occupations had provided a steady stream of information relating to military works and developments of all kinds. Even before the battle for Singapore had started, morale had become a serious problem. Troops were losing confidence in the commanders and in the prospects for relief. Large numbers of deserters could be seen in downtown Singapore or in the harbour areas trying to board ships for Australia, India or the Dutch East Indies.

Events on the mainland, the swift, relentless Japanese advance, forced Percival to order the withdrawal to the island rather earlier than he had planned, to avoid his forces there being overrun and defeated in detail.

The situation was actually even more precarious than Percival realised. Although he was not aware of it, the Japanese were making very good progress and believed that there was a real possibility that the entirety of Heath's III Corps could be cut off from the rest of Malaya Command and be forced to surrender, which would greatly reduce the strength available to protect

31. Coastal gun emplacement, Sentosa, Singapore. (Author's collection)

32. British optical range finder as issued to coastal artillery positions for identifying hostile ships, but for when the threat would come overland rather than from the sea. (Author's collection)

33. A 15in coastal gun on Singapore.

the island once the withdrawal was complete. Percival held a conference at Heath's headquarters and a programme for evacuation was agreed which would see the last troops cross the causeway to Singapore on 31 January.

The remaining searchlight and anti-aircraft assets on the mainland were promptly removed to the causeway area to give as much protection as possible to the withdrawing troops. An outer perimeter was also set up in and around Johore Bahru to ensure the security of the north end of the causeway and, hopefully, to gather stragglers heading away from the battle to the supposed relative safety of Singapore. In one of the few examples of a successful operation by Malaya Command, most of the troops in Johore were able to make their way to the causeway without being snarled up in traffic jams – no mean feat given the large

34. Japanese infantry storm into Johore Bahru.

numbers of men and vehicles involved, and the fact that so many had become detached from their units. By good fortune – and because the exhausted Japanese were in no condition to follow up as quickly as the Allies could retreat – the operation was completed by about 0600hrs on the 31st and the outer ring of the perimeter, consisting of 22nd Australian Brigade and the Gordon Highlanders, was able to withdraw through a final defensive line around the causeway held by the Argylls, now reduced to less than 300 all ranks. Shortly after 0800hrs the Argylls were played across by their last two pipers and the causeway was blown as soon as the last man had crossed over to Singapore

Planning for the defence of Singapore followed the same general pattern as the policy that had already failed in Malaya. In an effort to provide some strength everywhere, the troops were spread thinly all around the island. Singapore was divided into three coastal sectors and a reserve area.

The Western Area Command under General Bennett extended from a point just west of the mouth of Sungei Jurong on the south coast to a point half a mile east of the causeway then due south from there to Bukit Timah. Bennett's command included

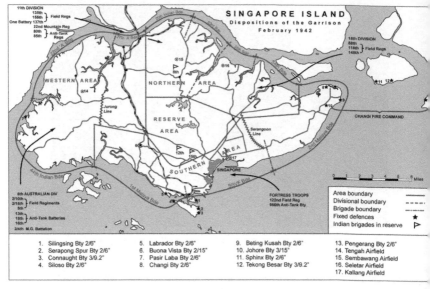

Singapore Island dispositions, February 1942.

his own 8th Division, including three field artillery regiments, three anti-tank regiments and nearly 2,000 newly arrived reinforcements from Australia. The latter had only been in Singapore for a little over a week and were far from being battle ready. The same applied to 44th Indian Brigade, now assigned to Bennett's command. They had arrived on 22 January, only partially trained, unaccustomed to the climate and less than fully fit after a lengthy voyage.

Heath's III Corps took responsibility for the Northern Area with the addition of the British 18th Division, most of which had only arrived on 29 December and without most of their vehicles, equipment and ammunition, which had been lost in a ship sunk by the Japanese. Southern Area, stretching eastwards along the coast from Sungei Jurong to a point 5 miles west of Changi at the eastern tip of the island, was entrusted to Major General Keith Simmons with a force made up of 1st and 2nd Malaya Brigades and Straits Settlements Volunteers. The 12th and 15th Indian Brigades were held as the command reserve in the Reserve Area, which stretched from Bukit Timah to Paya Lebar and included the vital Pierce and MacRitchie reservoirs.

The general state of confusion and disintegrating morale prevented any concerted effort to organise defences properly. It was now virtually impossible to find civilian labour at any price and most fortifications were being constructed by the troops who would be fighting in them. The work was hard, but not always effective since much of the terrain was not suitable for trenches and a lot of the positions that were erected consisted of breastworks with barbed wire, when it could be made available. Breastworks, if well made, can be effective against small arms fire but are of limited value against artillery and bombing, and are often vulnerable to attacks in the flanks or the rear. Much of the work that did continue had to be conducted at night, as did any major troop movements, for fear of Japanese air attacks; a great deal of the northern part of the island was now under direct observation from high ground and tall buildings in Johore, including the sultan's palace.

Air raids had diminished for a period after the start of the campaign as the Japanese concentrated on targets on the mainland, but started again in earnest on the night of 29/30 January. A force of fifty-one Hurricane fighters had arrived in January with a complement of twenty-four pilots, but however determined their efforts – and those of the few surviving Buffalo fighters' pilots who now had to struggle to familiarise themselves with a new aircraft – there was little they could do to prevent attacks. A second group of Hurricanes were dispatched from the carrier HMS *Indomitable* between 27 and 29 January and were dispersed to operate from airfields in Sumatra, but several of these were destroyed on the ground by Japanese bombing raids and others in engagements with Japanese fighters in the first couple of days after their arrival. From 12 January onward, the Japanese could mount bombing raids by day at little risk.

Although the mainland had been evacuated on 31 January, General Yamashita did not press on with an attack immediately. His troops had been fighting continuously for eight weeks and were exhausted. Men had become scattered from their units so had to be located and returned; ammunition stacks had to be replenished and assault craft had to be brought in before he could mount an operation. Although their ammunition supply was low, Yamashita was determined to allow the Allied troops no respite. As such, sporadic and relatively minor artillery bombardments started on 1 February, directed from observation posts on high ground and at least one observation balloon. Such balloons were rather anachronistic by 1942 but the Japanese had virtually complete control of the air so there was little threat of the balloon being shot down.

The Allied artillery was not silent, and sections (two guns) of various regiments were moved around the island (in the hope that the Japanese would not be able to identify their positions quickly enough to arrange counter-battery fire) to deliver harassing fire. They were, however, limited to no more than twenty rounds per day. This restriction had been imposed to preserve ammunition stocks for the main battle since Percival was planning for a struggle of three months, in the hope that a major relief operation could be mounted in that period. With stocks of 25-pounder and anti-aircraft ammunition already running low, Percival felt that he needed to retain as much of an ammunition reserve as possible as there was little prospect of replenishment for several weeks at least. The order would have unfortunate unintended consequences, for it was construed as a general policy for the entire battle rather than a temporary restriction to be observed until the Japanese attempted a landing. The absence of British air support and the firing restrictions allowed the Japanese to regroup and prepare their forces almost with impunity.

Remarkably, no effort had been made to arrange for observers to be left in Johore who could report on Japanese movements by wireless, and there was no realistic possibility of garnering such intelligence from local sources since the telephone lines to the island had been cut. Even if this had not been the case, it is not at all certain that any information provided by local people would have been taken seriously, nor that it would have been acted on. Deprived of aerial reconnaissance as well as any other form of intelligence material, the Allies were forced to rely on patrols crossing the strait to Johore by night in small boats. There seems to have been no sorties across the strait from the Western Area before 6 February, but there were a number from the Eastern Area, none of which reported any extensive movements of infantry or artillery concentrations. It was not until the night of the 6th that Bennett's Western Area headquarters was instructed to send patrols across the strait to investigate activity to the west of Johore.

35. Typical pre-war 'atap' house of the kind found in kampongs *(villages) the length and breadth of Malaya and Singapore. (Author's collection)*

36. *Typical pre-war shop-houses of the kind found throughout Malaya and Singapore. (Author's collection)*

On the night of 7/8th, patrols from 22nd Australian Brigade had managed to cross the strait and reconnoitred about 5 miles of coastline between Sungei Malayu and Sungei Pendas. They had identified a considerable concentration of Japanese infantry units, but little in the way of artillery and no landing craft at all; however, they had not been able to move much more than a mile inland and had been unable to penetrate as far north as Sungei Skudai. The landing craft were certainly being prepared for the assault, but not in the areas to which the patrols could penetrate.

By the morning of 8 February Malaya Command intelligence was confident that a major Japanese attack on the north-western coast between Sungei Berih and Kranji was imminent, but their conclusions were not shared with Bennett's headquarters until sometime after 1500hrs. Bennett made an immediate and urgent request for an aerial reconnaissance of what he assumed – rightly – to be the Japanese forming-up area, but there were simply no aircraft to be had, and even if there had been there was very little chance that a reconnaissance mission would have been successful in the face of Japanese air superiority. The best that could be done was to fire a number of speculative concentrations based on the information obtained by the patrols and reasonable deductions. None of this had any discernible impact on Japanese preparations.

THE BATTLEFIELD:
WHAT ACTUALLY HAPPENED?

Failure to stop Japanese Twenty-Fifth Army in Malaya did not mean they were undamaged by the campaign. Casualties among the infantry particularly had been considerable, though many of the tanks that had been put out of action had been repaired and returned to units by 8 February. The Japanese lines of communication had stretched beyond capacity despite use of captured vehicles. General Yamashita was forced to pause for a week in Johore to stockpile materials, get engineering equipment to the front and reorganise his units before making an attack.

His plans had to include a role for Guards Division. The division had not acquitted itself especially well in the campaign so far, and Yamashita's main assault would be conducted by the 5th and 18th Divisions, but the prestige of the Guards Division and the influence of their commanding officer at home obliged Yamashita to put them into the fight, so he decided to use them in an assault on the eastern aspect of the battle as well as the west. The attack was not redundant in that it would help to prevent the Allies from reinforcing the defenders in the Western Area, where the main attack would be pressed, but it would also reduce the availability of landing craft and other resources to support the 5th and 18th Divisions. In total, Yamashita had a force of about 30,000 men. He was heavily outnumbered, short of food and ammunition, and was not absolutely confident about the attitude of the commander of the Guards Division, Major General Nishimura.

A Desperate Situation

At first glance, Percival appears to have been in a relatively strong position. A wide stretch of water lay between him and the enemy, quite a lot of the coast was covered with mangrove swamp which would be virtually impassable to tanks or transport, and each passing day was an opportunity to add to the pillboxes and gun positions around the island, as well as giving a little more time to rest and reorganise his forces. In reality, his position was already desperate. His force of thirty-eight infantry battalions, three machine-gun battalions and nine field artillery regiments was much less than the sum of its parts. Huge amounts of equipment were lost in the campaign – not just materiel destroyed in combat, but large quantities that had been abandoned due to premature blowing of bridges, failures of transport or that had been captured by rapid Japanese advances. One Japanese unit was already using captured British artillery pieces before the attack on Singapore took place.

Many units had lost heavily during the retreat, and although some manpower shortages could be made up by transferring administrative staff, drivers, cooks and others to the rifle companies, the competence of the unit as a whole was undermined. Percival was further hampered by a determined lack of co-operation on the part of Sir Shenton Thomas and conflicting instructions from Wavell and London. On the one hand he was expected to carry on the fight to the last bullet, on the other he was required to prevent the Japanese from acquiring any supplies and equipment if the island should fall. These two objectives were mutually incompatible. If he was going to fight he would need all the arms, ammunition, food and other materiel that he could muster.

He also made a number of poor policy decisions. He put far too much faith in the sparse chain of fortified positions around the coast. There was a failure to use all of the assets available, including eighteen light tanks. The vehicles were lightly armed, poorly armoured and positively obsolete, but if they had been moved around the island extensively before the Japanese landing they might possibly have boosted confidence. His plan was to attempt to defend the island from any angle but still retain a large reserve to repel the invasion. However, he had inadequate plans or transport to bring the reserve into battle quickly or effectively, and he was further impeded by a lack of wireless equipment, much of which had been lost on the mainland and extensive damage had been done to the military and civil telephone lines through Japanese bombing and shelling. He had very real intelligence about the enemy's intentions and Japanese shelling forced the abandonment of all the airfields in the northern part of the island, though by the time the Japanese landed there were only ten Hurricanes and handful of Buffalo fighters still operational – hardly enough to deter bombing raids, let alone provide any support for the troops on the ground.

First Action

	7 February	Japanese troops seize Pulau Ubin and land on Singapore Island.
8 February		Japanese troops land on Singapore Island in considerable numbers.
		Japanese landing forces press inland to the village of Ama Keng.
	2200hrs	Battle commences in the Sarimbun beach area between Japanese forces and 22nd Brigade.

The first action of the battle for Singapore took place on the night of 7/8 February, when Japanese troops landed on Pulau Ubin, an island about 5 miles long lying in the eastern channel of the Johore Strait. Curiously, although the neighbouring island of Pulau Tekong Besar was garrisoned by 2/17th Dogra Battalion to protect the two coastal batteries there (Sphinx battery with two 6in guns and Tekong Besar battery with three 9.2in guns), Pulau Ubin does not seem to have figured in the general defence plan for Singapore at all. It was unprotected other than by patrols from the 4th Norfolks, which were immediately withdrawn to Changi.

From dawn onward shelling and air attacks increased steadily, with several air strikes being mounted on the positions held by 22nd Australian Brigade in Western Area. By the early afternoon the Japanese artillery bombardments had become more focused on headquarter assets and virtually all communications within the brigade area had been thoroughly disrupted by dusk. Both Bennett and Percival formed the opinion that this was not an indication of an immediate attack, but rather the beginning of

37. Restored 6in gun position at the excellent Siloso Fort Museum, Sentosa, Singapore. (Author's collection)

a prolonged bombardment that might last for some days before the Japanese attempted a landing. Neither were particularly concerned, believing that there would be opportunities to restore communications and repair defences. On account of this assumption, no special effort was made to disrupt Japanese preparations with artillery. This was not entirely irrational. Ammunition supplies were limited and would be required for infantry support once the battle was joined; furthermore, the lack of verifiable targets would mean that any artillery fire would be highly speculative and probably very wasteful.

Battle commenced in the Sarimbun beach area, when Australian troops of Brigadier Taylor's 22nd Brigade fired on landing craft and requisitioned civilian boats carrying elements of the Japanese 5th and 18th Divisions sometime after 2200hrs on 8 February.

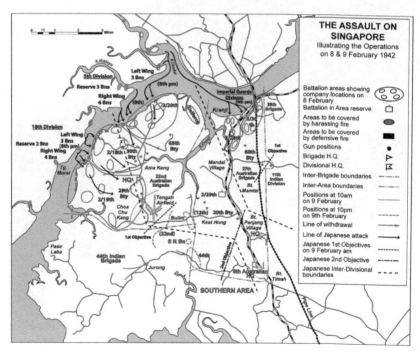

Assault on Singapore.

By midnight it had become apparent that the Japanese were attempting to land in considerable strength all along a wide front from Tanjong Murai to Tanjong Buloh. The first wave of over 4,000 infantry landed safely with good artillery support and was able to make decent headway through the gaps between the Australian positions, exploiting many small inlets and river mouths. Brigadier Taylor had issued orders that searchlights were not to be used until such time as the enemy were clearly engaged in a major landing, for fear that the lights would be put out of action almost as soon as they started operating. However, a large proportion of the lights that were available had already been disabled by artillery and mortar fire from Johore and from the Sarimbun beachhead, which the Japanese had secured in the first hour or so of the battle. The few that had survived were never put to use due, among other reasons, to the fact that communications between the searchlight units and the different battalion headquarters had been destroyed during the preliminary bombardment and air strikes.

Although fire plans had been made with a landing in mind, the disruption of signals made it impossible for the infantry battalions to call for the artillery support they required if the Japanese were to be slowed down let alone stopped on the beaches, but in fact the available support consisted of only three batteries (29th, 30th and 65th) and was not adequate to the task of delivering bombardments all along the brigade front, a distance of over 5 miles.

At different locations the landing forces suffered heavy casualties and in some places troops were only landed successfully after a fierce struggle, but the front was far too extensive to be held by a single brigade and the Japanese were able to secure the landing areas, infiltrate between the scattered posts along the coast and press inland toward the village of Ama Keng. This would develop a salient that would divide 22nd Brigade in two, with 2/18th Battalion and 2/20th Battalion to the north and 2/19th to the south. It would also threaten the position of the brigade headquarters, just a few hundred yards to the south of Ama Keng, and the position of 29th Battery only a further half mile south.

The Japanese made incredibly quick headway and caused a great deal of confusion, which was amplified by the absence of reliable communications within 22nd Brigade. A little before midnight, Brigadier Taylor was able to make some sense of the tactical picture and communicated his view to General Bennett's headquarters. His brigade reserve had been committed to the fight and he was convinced that the situation could only be retrieved by a major counter-attack at dawn. To this end, Bennett gave him command of another battalion (2/29th Australian), ordered fire on the Skudai estuary in Johore (which had been identified as a major route for Japanese reinforcements) and asked Percival's headquarters for all the air support that could be mustered. However, by this stage the RAF's offensive capacity had been reduced to a mere fourteen aircraft (four Fairey Swordfish and ten Hurricanes) still based on the island.

Bennett had formed a 'Special Reserve battalion' of over 400 men from Royal Army Service Corps personnel and others and at 0300hrs he put them and elements of 2/4th Machine Gun Battalion under Taylor's command. The reserve battalion had been formed over the previous week and had had little time for training or to develop the cohesion that is vital for effective infantry units, but in any case, the forces now at Taylor's disposal were completely inadequate to the task of mounting a major counter-attack over a front of some miles. Although Taylor's tactical instinct was probably correct – that an immediate counter-attack would have been the preferable course of action – it was not a realistic proposition under the circumstances. Several units and sub-units of his brigade were at risk of being surrounded, and he did not have sufficient strength to secure their positions.

A Force Divided

0100hrs	22nd Brigade forced to retreat to the point of not being able to present a united opposition.
0300hrs	All three battalions ordered to retire to pre-planned fall-back positions.
0500hrs	Reinforcements arrive for 22nd Brigade.
0715hrs	2/18th Battalion attacked at Ama Keng.
0930hrs	2/18th Battalion forced back to RAF Tengah.
2200hrs	Firing ceases; first elements of 4th Regiment of the Japanese Guards Division land.

In a matter of a few hours the Japanese managed to sever communications between 22nd and 27th Australian Brigades. 22nd Brigade was forced to retreat and by 0100hrs on 9 February they were unable to present a united opposition to the Japanese advance, now supported by a second wave of troops landing in the north-west. Elements of 22nd Brigade became isolated and were forced to surrender despite Taylor committing such reserves as he had to hand. Fighting was fierce everywhere along the front. Casualties and prisoners reduced Australian 2/18th Battalion to below half numbers. By 0300hrs each of the three battalion commanders had given orders for their units to retire to pre-planned fall-back positions. The actions through the night of 9 February rather encapsulate the story of the whole Malayan campaign: a pattern of Japanese forces infiltrating between Allied units and making daring attacks, obliging Allied units to retire to another position, which in turn forces neighbouring units to conform to a new 'line' and supporting units to withdraw in order to make space for new arrivals. During the campaign on the mainland, repeated withdrawals had had the apparent value of allowing units to regroup and sometimes gain a little time to prepare new positions while the Japanese reorganised for a further advance. Now that the battle had been carried on to Singapore itself there was simply no physical space for manoeuvres of that ilk.

Although elements of 2/18th Battalion managed to make their way to their new position at Ama Keng, they were attacked again a short while after sunrise (about 0715hrs). Despite hard fighting and a counter-attack in conjunction with the engineers of 2/10th Field Company, the battalion could not hold their position and by 0930hrs had been forced back to the airfield of RAF Tengah. Meanwhile, most of 2/19th Battalion had become seriously disrupted by near-continual combat through the night. Many of the troops had become detached from the battalion and were turning up as far back as the 8th Division headquarters area at Bukit Timah, some 3 miles or more east of Tengah. The remaining battalion of Taylor's 22nd Brigade, 2/20th, had been heavily engaged by overwhelming numbers all along its front and had been forced to retire from its positions in the Namazhe estate and then separated from the remainder of the brigade by Japanese troops moving inland along the line of the Sungei Sarimbun. Shortly after dawn, the battalion attempted to rejoin the brigade by moving south toward Ama Keng only to find that their path was blocked by strong Japanese forces. The battalion was now broken up into small parties, some of which moved east to cross Sungei Kranji then headed south. Some elements were able to make their way to the brigade headquarters, now at Bulim, but all of the battalions had sustained heavy losses through a mixture of combat and disruption, and the brigade was no longer an effective force.

Although Bennett had authorised reinforcements for Taylor's command, the battalion allocated, 2/29th, had not been in a position to move immediately to his aid. Some of the battalion were in a position on the Woodlands Road about halfway between Mandai and Bukit Timah; a considerable portion was engaged in training elsewhere. It took some time to concentrate the battalion and consequently they did not arrive at Tengah until about an hour before dawn on 9 February. Taylor now had three units from outside his own brigade under his command: the Jind Battalion from 44th Indian Brigade, 2/29th from 27th Australian Brigade and the Special Reserve Battalion that Bennett had assembled over the previous week. He deployed the Jinds and 2/29th on a line running from just north of Tengah to the north of Sungei Berih, where one company of 2/19th Battalion was still in position at the village of Choa Chu Kang. Taylor clearly intended to reorganise his own battalions behind these units, but was given the additional task of mounting a counter-attack by 2/29th, with the intention of pushing the enemy back beyond Ama Keng. The proposition that one infantry battalion would be able to throw back the scale of force that had already put an entire brigade out of the battle was clearly unsustainable, but was not put to the test. By mid-morning, well before the time set for the proposed attack, Taylor's position was threatened by Japanese units that had moved east and then south to compromise his right flank.

Brigadier Paris' 12th Indian Brigade were brought in to reinforce the Australians, but communications with 8th Division headquarters at Bukit Timah were now non-existent and Taylor had no means of ascertaining General Bennett's intentions or the condition of neighbouring formations. Thus he and Paris agreed that 12th Brigade should deploy between Bulim and Keat Hong at the northern end of the Jurong Line – a series of half-prepared positions running north from the head of Sungei Jurong. Aware that 22nd Brigade could now be in danger of being cut off either by direct attacks on its own positions around Bulim and Tengah, or if the Japanese were able to dislodge 12th Brigade, Taylor decided to rationalise his line by adopting a position running south from Bulim to the Jurong Road, thus conforming to the Jurong Line. By the time the move was initiated, the Japanese, like the Australians, had been in near-continuous action for more than fifteen hours and were now tired and short of ammunition, and the nature of their attack – infiltrating between the Australian positions – meant that several of their battalions had become scattered and disorganised. Although Taylor's troops were subjected to several air strikes and some artillery fire, they were able to take up their new positions largely unimpeded and some progress could be made toward regrouping the battalions. Although his actions were unauthorised – and he received a stern warning from Bennett accordingly – Taylor had had little choice but to retire if his brigade was not to be destroyed, but his withdrawal was completely contrary to the orders received from his senior officer and to the general principles on which the battle was supposed to be fought. The only hope for success was to fight a battle of attrition that would inflict so many casualties on the Japanese that they would be forced to withdraw, regroup and make a new attempt. With hindsight it is easy to conclude that the battle for Singapore had already been lost some time before, but Taylor's decisions ceded ground to the Japanese at no cost at all – and not only within his own sector of responsibility. The neighbouring formation, 44th Indian Brigade under Brigadier Ballentine, would be in danger of becoming isolated if it was not re-deployed to take account of Taylor's movements.

When General Percival visited Bennett's headquarters on the afternoon of the 9th they had given some thought to the possibility that 44th Brigade might be concentrated – the troops were dispersed in defensive positions from Jurong to Pasir Laba – and make an attack on the southern flank of the Japanese forces engaged with 22nd Brigade. The idea had been abandoned almost as soon as it was suggested, though it is hard to see why. The positions occupied by 44th Brigade were clearly going to have to be abandoned unless the Japanese could be repelled and there could hardly be a better opportunity. The Japanese were tired, scattered and disorganised from hard fighting; even if the attack made little progress it would allow a bit of breathing space for 22nd Brigade, and 44th Brigade would be able to attack the enemy when they did not have the benefit of armoured support. However, instead of making a bold move that might have a positive outcome, Ballentine was ordered to move his brigade eastward to take up positions on the southern end of the Jurong with 22nd Brigade; 12th Brigade held the northern portion and 15th Brigade was in reserve to their rear, screening the crucial supply dumps around Bukit Timah.

The rapid progress of the Japanese against 22nd Brigade had consequences elsewhere. Of the three battalions of the Australian 27th Brigade (Brigadier Maxwell), one (2/29th) was assigned to support 22nd Brigade, but by dusk the left flank of the remaining battalions (2/26th and 2/30th, deployed around Kranji and the causeway respectively) was under threat. Maxwell wanted to move 2/26th to prevent the Japanese from crossing the Sungei Kranji, but instead was given permission to use two companies to guard the Sungei Peng Siang, a tributary to the Kranji. One of these was the reserve company of the 2/26th, but the other was to be a more ad hoc body drawn from the other companies in the battalion, thus weakening each of them. Throughout the day, the brigade area had been subjected to increasingly heavy artillery fire and air strikes, which, though they inflicted relatively light casualties, damaged or destroyed a good deal of transport and, more importantly, damaged defences and thoroughly disrupted brigade communications. Firing ceased about an hour after dusk, sometime around 2200hrs, as the first elements of the 4th Regiment of the Japanese Guards Division landed.

A Stout Defence

10 February

2/28th and 2/30th Battalions withdraw inland toward Mandai in the early hours.

Tank unit attached to the Japanese Guards Regiment lands in Kranji and deployed on Woodlands Road.

Commonwealth forces lose the Jurong Line.

Wavell visits Singapore for the final time and orders a counter-attack to retake the Jurong Line.

The Japanese regroup most of 5th Division around Tengah Airfield and 18th Division on the Jurong Road.

This time the Japanese did not make the kind of progress to which they had become accustomed through most of the campaign. Several of the assault craft became separated from the main body and a number were sunk. Well-handled machine-gun and mortar fire inflicted considerable casualties on the run-in to the shore, where the attackers then encountered burning oil and petrol that had been prepared for in advance. Although losses had been heavy and the hold on the shore was not extensive, the Guards initially struggled to hang on in the face of a stout Australian defence, but as reinforcements arrived they were able to gain the initiative and after some heavy fighting were able to force 2/26th to a position about a quarter of a mile from the shoreline. This allowed for one of the few genuinely successful attempts at denying the Japanese the material prizes of Singapore to be carried out. Through the night an Australian engineering officer charged with destroying the large supplies in the Woodlands fuel tank area found himself without the necessary explosives, so he simply opened the taps and let the contents flow freely into the strait. Whether by accident or design, the fuel was ignited by small arms fire and as the tide pushed it into the streams and swamps around Kranji the burning fuel caused extensive casualties among Japanese troops.

Maxwell knew that 22nd Brigade had been roughly handled by the Japanese and was concerned that his own brigade would now become isolated. Major Oakes, who had been given command of both 2/28th and 2/30th Battalions to hold back the Japanese and to ensure the destruction of the Woodlands fuel tanks, concluded that his men were now in danger of being overrun and started to withdraw inland, away from the Kranji area and toward Mandai in the early hours of 10 February. This naturally ceded the shoreline to the west of the causeway and passed the tactical initiative to the Japanese at a critical juncture.

Impressed by the tenacity of the Australians, the commander of the Guards Division, General Nishimura, had asked permission from General Yamashita's headquarters to withdraw his men and make a new landing the following day further to the west. As soon as it became apparent that the Australians were withdrawing, any such plan was abandoned in favour of pursuing the original objectives. Instead of having to either mount a supporting attack to relieve

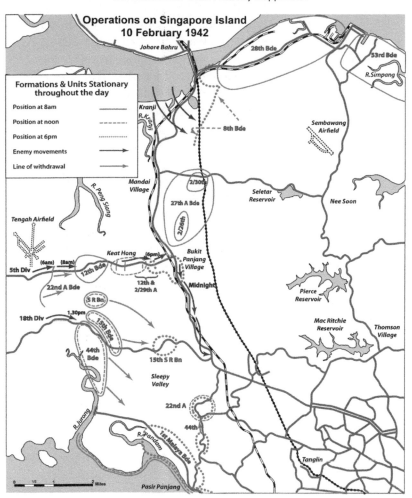

Operations of 10 February 1942.

the Guards detachments to the west of the causeway or even withdraw them from their small beachhead, Yamashita could now expand his position on the northern shore of Singapore. Tactically, this restricted the freedom of action of Bennett's command and threatened the left flank of Heath's III Corps in the Eastern Area.

It also gave Yamashita the opportunity to exploit one of his most important assets. The tank unit attached to the Guards Division was now floated across the Johore Strait, landed in the Kranji area and deployed on to the Woodlands Road. The Guards Division could have seized the moment and made a thrust toward Singapore city, but failed to do so; however, the Allied situation was now positively perilous. Bennett's Jurong Line had been compromised on its northern flank and the Australian division was now separated from 11th Indian Division in the naval base area. 11th Division headquarters were not made aware of the situation until about an hour before dawn. Realising that there was now a space of more than 2 miles between his own troops and the Australians that was completely unguarded against the Japanese, the divisional commander, General Key, contacted Western Area Command to ask that the situation be stabilised, only to be told that there were no units to be spared. This was the simple truth; all of the units in Western Area had suffered considerable losses, were already engaged, were too far away or, in the case of 15th Brigade, were required to provide support for units in contact with the enemy. Key decided that the only hope of restoring the situation was to secure the high ground overlooking the strait, and thus ordered 8th Indian Brigade to make a counter-attack to the north and west, and asked Brigadier Maxwell to ensure that Mandai village was occupied in order to protect the flank of 8th Brigade as they moved forward.

Retreats

Throughout the 10th some semblance of order was achieved across the front, which now extended from the high ground to the east of Sungei Mandai, where 8th Indian Brigade had made some progress at heavy cost to Mandai village. Here 27th Brigade held positions overlooking the Woodlands Road, while 8th Indian Brigade progressed to a point between Bulim and Keat Hong, then south to the headwaters of the Sungei

Jurong. In just two days of fighting, the Japanese had already taken about one-third of Singapore Island, and now the situation took a marked turn for the worse. The nearest thing to a natural defensive line between the Japanese Army and Singapore city was the Jurong Line, which ran along a really rather minor ridge between the sources of the Kranji and Jurong rivers. The positions were not especially strong, but they were a good deal better than nothing and – in some areas at least – gave the Allied troops reasonable fields of fire for machine guns and anti-tank guns. Additionally, the line was relatively short and strongly manned by 22nd Brigade, 44th Brigade and 12th Brigade.

Concerned that the Japanese would be able to seize the supply dumps around Bukit Timah and the reservoirs, and deprive his command of food, ammunition and water, Percival had drawn up a plan for a strong defensive inner perimeter with zones and tasks allotted to specified formations. Brigadier Maxwell received the instructions and then totally misunderstood them. Rather than seeing them as instructions for a planned withdrawal to the new line at the last possible moment, he and his staff construed Percival's orders as instructions to retire at the earliest opportunity. Consequently, Maxwell set out to examine the new positions with a view to allotting roles to the units under his command. En route he visited General Bennett's headquarters to inform his commander of his progress only to be told – in no uncertain terms – that he had utterly misread the situation. Bennett was furious with his subordinate, but, incomprehensibly, did nothing at all to remedy the situation.

By withdrawing his brigade, Maxwell had thoroughly compromised the Jurong Line. Brigadier Paris' 12th Indian Brigade, severely weakened from action during the retreat to Singapore, now came under sustained pressure from the Japanese. Unable to establish contact with the Australian 27th Brigade on his right flank or with Western Area headquarters, and concerned that a Japanese advance to Bukit Timah would isolate his brigade, Paris decided to pull back to Bukit Panjang village.

Paris' actions were unavoidable if his units, now including elements of the Australian 2/29th Battalion, were not to be cut off, but his withdrawal left two other brigades, 44th and 15th, vulnerable to attacks on their flanks. By early afternoon a mixture of heavy fire from the Japanese and an unfounded report that a neighbouring British battalion had withdrawn caused various elements of 44th Brigade to make an unauthorised retreat that Brigadier Ballentine was able to bring to a halt, but only at the cost of concentrating his men at Pasir Panjang. At this point he was able to make contact with Southern Area headquarters and was told to take his brigade to a location at the Ulu Pandan, about 1 mile south of Bukit Timah.

The entire Jurong Line plan was now utterly redundant. To the south, 1st Malaya Brigade (Brigadier Williams) was now exposed on its northern flank and was obliged to retire to Pasir Panjang on the south coast, and in the Northern Area, Brigadier Coates' 15th Brigade was forced to retire to a new position on the Jurong Road, where they were joined by the Australian Special Reserve Battalion. Although the Jurong Line was far from being a thoroughly prepared position, it had been reconnoitred, some fire plans had been made and some defences erected. It was certainly the only feasible defensive line to the west of Singapore city, but it had been effectively abandoned by about 1800hrs on 10 February. After less than two days of fighting, nearly one-third of Singapore Island was in Japanese hands and several of Percival's brigades – 12th, 15th and 44th Indian and 22nd and 27th Australian – had suffered substantial casualties and were close to exhaustion.

The fighting had taken its toll on the Japanese as well, but they were now firmly established on the island. The nature of the terrain and the infiltration tactics employed had resulted in several units becoming quite scattered, but by the evening of the 10th the Japanese had been able to regroup most of 5th Division and some tanks around Tengah Airfield. At the same time, 18th Division concentrated on the Jurong Road about 3 miles west of Bukit Timah and both formations were ready to renew the fight.

On the afternoon of 10 February, Wavell, making his final visit to Singapore, met Bennett at Western Area headquarters and was informed that the Jurong Line had been taken; though to a great extent it had really been abandoned. Wavell ordered Bennett to mount a counter-attack to recover the Jurong positions at the

38. Forest and mountain terrain in eastern Malaya. (Author's collection)

39. A jungle creek. Although few Japanese soldiers had received any jungle-warfare training, they proved adept at infiltrating Allied positions by following small streams like this one in western Singapore. (Author's collection)

40. Gen. Wavell in Singapore inspecting coastal guns, November 1941.

earliest opportunity. If successful, it would provide a focus for
the defence of the rest of the island and a barrier behind which
the infantry units could be regrouped, replenished and rotated,
and where artillery batteries could be sited. Without the Jurong
Line there was no realistic prospect of halting the Japanese and a
plan of sorts was formulated in which 22nd Brigade to the south,
15th Brigade in the centre and 12th Brigade to the north, with the
support of two regiments of field artillery and with 44th Brigade in
reserve, would regain the Jurong Line. The first step of the attack
would take place before 1800hrs that day. The problem with the
scheme was that none of the formations involved were fit for an
advance at all. By chance – and nothing more – they happened
to be in relatively convenient locations for the tasks allotted, but

losses in men, transport and communications, exhaustion and local shortages of ammunition and water meant that there was no realistic prospect of mounting a successful attack without bringing large numbers of fresh troops into the battle. Additionally, the plan gave precious little thought to the practical difficulties of moving a large proportion of the attacking force through the night and seemingly no consideration at all to what actions the Japanese might have in mind.

Relentless

	0000hrs	Japanese troops secure Bukit Timah junction.
	0300hrs	18th Division advance toward Bukit Timah.
11 February	0530hrs	15th Brigade ordered to counter-attack and break contact with the enemy by going cross country toward 22nd Brigade.
	1300hrs	Bennett's counter-attack to retake Bukit Timah abandoned.

Around 0300hrs on 11 February elements of 18th Division, with a modest amount of armoured support, advanced from the Tengah area toward Bukit Timah along the Jurong Road.

Around 0530hrs Brigadier Coates, aware that 15th Brigade was in danger of being completely surrounded and overwhelmed, gave orders to cancel the counter-attack and to break contact with the enemy. This was easier said than done. Japanese advances meant that much of the Jurong Road was now impassable and Coates ordered his remaining units to strike out cross-country toward the positions of 22nd Brigade.

To the north, troops from 5th Division, with a strong armoured element, had advanced from their concentration area and despite a strong stand by 2/29th, were able to reach Bukit Panjang village and then turn south toward Bukit Timah. At about 2230hrs they encountered the Argyll and Sutherland Highlanders, who put up a fierce fight but could not hope to stop a column of fifty or so tanks.

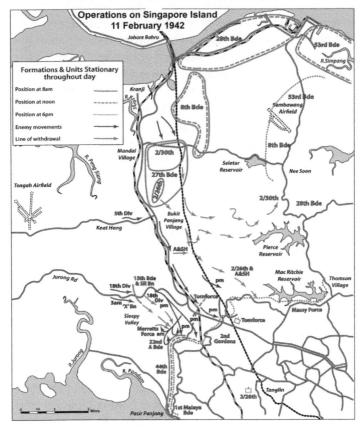

Operations of 11 February 1942.

By midnight Japanese troops had secured the Bukit Timah junction, cutting communications to 15th Brigade, but did not press on into Singapore city, though there was really precious little to stop them.

By this time several units had simply been destroyed and others so badly damaged that they were increasingly being formed into ad hoc units. Breakdown of discipline was also becoming a problem, with considerable numbers of personnel – chiefly British and Australian – roaming around in search of loot or any means of escape.

Now that Bukit Timah was in Japanese hands, they were well positioned to advance westward through the central part of the island toward the Pierce and MacRitchie reservoirs. The defenders had already lost the bulk of their stores when the Bukit Timah supply dumps were overrun, now their very limited water supplies would be under threat as well. Early on the 11th, Bennett had ordered another counter-attack to retake Bukit Timah, but by 1300hrs this attempt had been abandoned as impractical since by this time a large proportion of both 5th and 18th Divisions – with a large number of tanks – had occupied the area. There was intensive fighting and heavy casualties on both sides, but the Japanese were not to be budged.

To the north, in the causeway area, the Japanese Guards Division made rather slower progress than 5th and 18th Divisions in the south and west, but had advanced along the line of the Sungei Mandai toward Mandai Ridge, threatening the southern flank of 8th Brigade and putting pressure on the left flank of 27th Brigade.

The battle was clearly going very badly for the Allies, but Yamashita was faced with serious problems of his own. Ostensibly his tanks had stopped at Bukit Timah because they had reached their objective, but Japanese units had repeatedly exceeded objectives during the peninsula campaign. Although Yamashita had paused for a week in Johore before making his attack, the efforts of the preceding weeks had exhausted his troops and his supplies. To some extent the rations situation could be eased by seizing food from shops and homes, but that was hardly a reliable approach to feeding his army. Other shortages, and especially of tank and small arms ammunition, could only be addressed by bringing materiel to the front (though there was no great stock anywhere in the peninsula) or by bringing the battle to a conclusion. Even so, it was clear from the Allied perspective that the battle could not continue very much longer. Yamashita saw the situation in the same terms and he now called on Percival to give up the fight. Percival forwarded the message to Wavell, saying that although he had no way of communicating with the

Japanese commander, he had no intention of surrendering at this juncture. All the same, he issued orders to destroy military installation and materiel to prevent it falling to the enemy. Under the circumstances, this was a perfectly sensible approach, but it further undermined morale among the troops and the civilian population. Denying materiel to the enemy was a clear indication that surrender would be offered in the very near future, so what was the value of continuing the fight at all?

Last Stand

12	0800hrs	8th Brigade come under attack by Japanese.
		Perimeter formed by the Allies, but very congested area.
13 February		Combat continues throughout the day.
	1430hrs	Percival calls a conference at his headquarters to discuss battle prospects.
14	0830hrs	1st Malaya Brigade attacked.
	1600hrs	1st Malaya Brigade forced back to the Brickworks.
15 February	0930hrs	Percival calls a conference at his headquarters.
	1130hrs	Percival sends deputation to make contact with the Japanese to arrange terms of surrender.
	1810hrs	Percival signs the capitulation document.

At about 0800hrs on 12 February, 8th Brigade came under attack and for a while the Japanese were close to breaking through toward Nee Soon village and the Sembawang Airfield, only 2 miles from the naval base. The situation was eventually restored by a spirited counter-attack by 2/9th Gurkhas from the 28th Brigade. Even so, the situation was critical here as well as in the Western Areas and Percival now decided it was time to withdraw all forces from the Northern and Eastern Areas and to form a defensive perimeter around the city. He envisaged a roughly hemispherical, nearly 30-mile long line that would stretch from Pasir Panjang in the west to the race course, then east to Thompson village and Bidadari, then south to Geylang and finally south-west to the coast at the Singapore Swimming Club.

At noon, 11th and 18th Divisions began to move to their allotted positions, which was achieved with little interference from the enemy other than an attack from Japanese tanks at the Nee Soon/Mandai Road junction. Elsewhere, 22nd Brigade – now under the command of Brigadier Varley – had repelled several attacks but was clearly at risk of becoming isolated and withdrew successfully to their perimeter position, which forced 44th Brigade and 1st Malaya Brigade to adjust their own positions or leave their flanks 'in the air'.

By early morning on the 13th the perimeter had been formed, but the area it described was now dreadfully congested. A steady tide of refugees had increased the population of Singapore city to about 1 million people and the concentration of service personnel and materiel within the perimeter was so great that there was hardly a space that did not constitute a legitimate military target for Japanese artillery and aircraft.

Combat continued throughout the day, including a determined action at Bukit Chandu on Pasir Panjang Ridge in which Lieutenant Adnan Bin Saidi won a posthumous Military Cross for his gallant efforts; however, the Japanese made modest but significant advances in several sectors, forcing the retreat of 44th Indian and 1st Malaya Brigades that night. At a 1030hrs meeting with Sir Shenton Thomas, the colonial governor, Percival made it clear that he still intended to carry on the fight, but the defensive perimeter was already under threat.

At 1430hrs on the 13th Percival called his subordinates to a conference at his headquarters at Fort Canning to discuss the prospects of the battle. Food supplies were now down to about seven days' worth, but there were still reasonable amounts of ammunition available, though the anti-aircraft batteries were running rather low. None of those present expressed any confidence that a counter-attack was a feasible proposition.

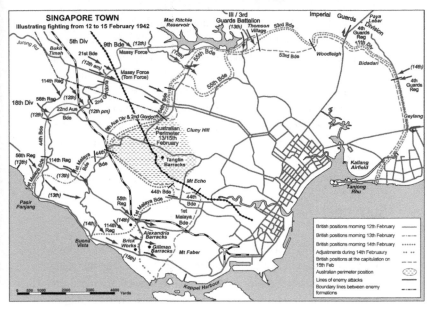

Singapore town.

Many of the front-line units were exhausted and a number had received little training and – especially 18th Division – no opportunity to adjust to the climate since they had arrived so recently. Although Bennett and Heath were in favour of surrendering, Percival maintained that the situation '… though undoubtedly grave, was not hopeless', and decided to continue the battle. It is difficult, if not impossible, to see what hope Percival thought there might be. The Japanese were on the island in great strength with plenty of tanks, they had total air and sea superiority, their morale was high and they held the tactical initiative in every sector of the front. Percival was well aware that there was no relief force en route to Singapore, and there was no realistic possibility of holding out beyond a couple of days at most. Even if the arrival of a powerful relief force had been imminent, the power of the Japanese at sea and in the air would almost certainly have prevented it being disembarked and brought into action.

At 0830hrs on the 14th, 1st Malaya Brigade had come under attack and, though this was repelled, by 1600hrs they had been forced back to the Brickworks only a mile or so west of Mount Faber, which overlooked the western edge of the city. Although there were Australian artillery units in the area which could have provided support, General Bennett had given strict orders that Australian guns were only to fire in support of Australian troops due to the growing ammunition shortage. Clearly this was not going to be of any help if the battle as a whole was lost so it is difficult to see what Bennett could hope to achieve by conserving ammunition.

Surrender

Although he was inclined to continue the fight, Percival realised that the end was in sight and that there was a limit to the value of further resistance, so he sent a signal to Wavell outlining the situation and asking for permission to seek terms when conditions deteriorated. Wavell's reply was far from helpful:

> You must continue to inflict maximum damage on the enemy for as long as possible by house-to-house fighting if necessary. Your action in tying down enemy and inflicting casualties may have vital influence in other theatres. Fully appreciate your situation but continued action essential.
>
> Major General Woodburn Kirby, *The War Against Japan*, HMSO, 1957

Clearly Wavell did not 'fully appreciate' the situation at all. Had he done, he would have understood that the campaign was over; that Percival's troops could achieve nothing by fighting on and that the plight of the civilian population was becoming desperate. Furthermore, fighting to the bitter end would have no appreciable effect on the Japanese in other theatres. Hong Kong had already fallen, the Japanese were making good progress in Burma and the Philippines and the war in China would not be greatly affected by transferring the relatively small numbers of troops in the Twenty-Fifth Army.

At 0930hrs on the 15th, Percival held another conference with his senior commanders, the Director General of Civil Defence and the Inspector General of Police. He was informed that shelling and bombing had caused extensive damage to the reservoirs and the distribution system, and that water supplies would last for forty-eight hours at best, and more likely only half that. Percival now accepted that there was no value to maintaining a defence since the Japanese were clearly capable of breaking his line at any point and decided that the only options were an immediate counter-attack or to surrender. His commanders' opinions on a counter-attack had not changed since the previous meeting. Although there were still ample quantities of small arms ammunition, there was little for the field artillery, almost none for the anti-aircraft batteries and a shortage of mortar bombs for the infantry battalions. Additionally, the stamina and the morale of the combat troops was causing concern, as was the now widespread failure of discipline among other personnel. Percival could have chosen to follow Wavell's orders and pressed his commanders to fight for every street and house. This would unquestionably have led to massive casualties among the residents as well as the combatants, but close combat of that nature tends to benefit the defenders, who have to be driven out of their positions by artillery and costly close attacks. It also demands the expenditure of very large amounts of ordnance, and Yamashita felt that he had neither the men nor the ammunition to conduct such a battle. He described his situation thus:

My Attack on Singapore was a bluff – a bluff that worked. I had 30,000 men and was outnumbered three to one. I knew that if I had to fight for long for Singapore I would be beaten. That is why the surrender had to be at once. I was very frightened all the time that the British would discover our numerical weakness and lack of supplies and force me into disastrous street fighting.

P. Elphick, *Singapore: The Pregnable Fortress*, London, 1985

In this respect Yamashita's analysis of the situation was cautious or even pessimistic. The ground force available to the Allied commander was unquestionably much greater than the Twenty-Fifth Army in number, but most of the troops had been engaged in a long retreat that had caused the loss of a great deal of their equipment and, perhaps more significantly, of any confidence that they were capable of defeating the Japanese on the battlefield. Allied troops could be fairly certain that any aircraft overhead were likely to belong to the enemy and could be utterly confident that if they heard tanks in the distance, they would be hostile ones. Moreover, if Yamashita's ammunition supply was limited, Percival's was not really much better. The shells, grenades and bullets may have existed, but there was no means of getting them to where they needed to be.

Percival was also obliged to consider the civilian population. Regardless of Churchill's cable to Wavell urging him to reject any thought of sparing the civilians, the practical reality was that there was something in the region of a million people concentrated in just a few square miles. If Yamashita was to adopt a policy of shelling and bombing the Allies into surrender the death toll would be horrendous. Percival had no reason to assume that the Japanese were so short of ammunition that this would not be a viable proposition. Even if Yamashita did not choose a policy of bombardment, Percival was all too aware that with the major reservoirs either captured or damaged, there would soon be a drastic shortage of water.

With Percival's own troops short on supplies of all kinds, increasing evidence of a breakdown in discipline and with no prospect of relief, Churchill and Wavell's instructions to fight on to the very last were utterly unrealistic. Although there was a still a huge reservoir of men on hand, there was no means of organising them into anything like a viable force. Many had lost or abandoned their rifles; quite a large number of air force and navy personnel had never been issued with a weapon in the first place and many had had little weapons training, let alone

41. *The Japanese victory parade in Fullerton Square, Singapore, 17 February 1942.*

tactical training of any kind. Large numbers of men from infantry battalions had become detached from their units – some quite deliberately in the hope of escaping by ship or simply to take cover until the fighting came to an end. Men from the other branches of service had come to the same idea, but even those who had remained with their units were at a loss. A great many of the artillery units had lost some or all of their guns during the retreat and those which had kept their guns had little or nothing in the way of ammunition.

With the decision to surrender accepted by all of his senior staff, Percival started the process of capitulation. At about 1130hrs he sent a deputation consisting of a staff officer, an interpreter and the colonial secretary to make contact with the Japanese to arrange terms. They came back with instructions that Percival

THE FORD FACTORY

What is now called the 'Old Ford Motor Factory', but in the past was known simply as 'The Ford Factory', was the first Ford assembly plant in Asia. Completed just a few months before the Japanese invasion, it was the scene of Percival's surrender to Yamashita. During the occupation it was used by Nissan for the assembly of vehicles for the occupation forces. Ford continued to use the building from 1947 to 1980 and since 2006 it has been a museum and archive storage facility for the National Archives of Singapore.

should make his way to meet Yamashita at the Singapore Ford Factory at Bukit Timah and that the flag of Japan should be raised on the Cathay building, the tallest edifice in the city, to show that the battle was over. Yamashita was not interested in discussing terms; he wanted an immediate and unconditional surrender. The discussions lasted less than an hour and at 1810hrs Percival signed the capitulation document.

AFTER THE BATTLE

It is often easy – or at least tempting – to assume that any major defeat was a foregone conclusion. The failure of successive British governments to take a realistic approach to defence in the Far East went a long way toward making the fall of Singapore inevitable. Even in the last days of the campaign there was a general tendency to ignore the practicalities of the situation. This signal from Churchill to Wavell exemplifies that tendency:

> I think you ought to realise the way we view the situation in Singapore. It was reported to cabinet by the CIGS (Chief of the Imperial General Staff – Sir Alan Brooke) that Percival has over 100,000 men, of whom 33,000 are British and 17,000 Australian. It is doubtful whether the Japanese have so many in the whole Malay Peninsula … In these circumstances and in a well-contested battle they should destroy them. There must at this stage be no thought of saving the troops or sparing the population. The battle must be fought to the bitter end at all costs. The 18th Division has a chance to make its name in history. Commanders and senior officers should die with their troops. The honour of the British Army is at stake.
>
> Major General Woodburn Kirby, *The War Against Japan*,
> HMSO, 1957

The cable shows Churchill's complete misunderstanding of the entire situation. Apart from the fact that he seems to have retained some confidence in the ideas of racial superiority in disregarding the Indian, Malay and Chinese service personnel, he had seemingly failed to grasp that the Japanese had been able to seize and retain their initiative due to better training, better leadership, better air support, their daring use of armour and a better understanding of what could and could not be achieved on the battlefield. None of these issues could be remedied simply by demanding a 'do or die' attitude. Defeat in the air meant that movement by day was extremely vulnerable to Japanese air strikes. Since neither Allied fighter strength nor anti-aircraft capacities presented very much of a challenge, Japanese pilots could afford to take their time seeking targets of opportunity. On the ground, the Allies had no real answer to Japanese armour. Yamashita's tanks may have been old-fashioned, lightly armoured and under-gunned, but the Allies had lost a great many anti-tank guns during the campaign, and even if the guns had been replaced the general approach to training had been so basic that most units had very little idea of how to deal with an armoured threat.

Percival went to The Ford Factory ostensibly to seek terms, though in practice he must have been aware that neither he nor Yamashita really had much room to manoeuvre. Realistically, Yamashita could only accept an unconditional surrender and Percival had nothing else to offer.

Percival's surrender was unconditional, though not strictly speaking, without terms, since there were a number of practical issues to be addressed. Neither Percival nor Yamashita had effective communications with all of their units, so a ceasefire deadline was set for 2030hrs to allow news of the surrender to be relayed to units out of radio contact. The surrender document explicitly required Percival to ensure that all military materiel – arms, ammunition, supplies of all kinds, transport, papers, ships and aircraft – was surrendered undamaged immediately. Yamashita accepted Percival's word that there were no aircraft

42. Lt Gen. Percival and party en route to surrender Singapore to the Japanese.

or ships left in Allied hands, but in fact he had already given instructions that all heavy artillery and documents were to be destroyed before 1600hrs.

Clearly there was already a good deal of disorder in the streets with soldiers and civilians looting shops and homes across the city. It would be some time before Japanese troops could be deployed all over the city, so Percival was allowed to retain 1,000 armed men to maintain law and order pending Japanese takeover.

Percival can certainly be counted among the losers in any examination of the 1941–42 campaign. To a considerable degree the dice were heavily loaded against him from the outset. An inexplicable tide of political and diplomatic constraints prevented him from taking positive courses of action from the very beginning of the campaign. Although a plan (Operation Matador) had been formulated to slow the Japanese advance in one of the few real 'choke' positions, diplomatic and political considerations conspired with poor communications and a lack of clarity to prevent the operation being put into action in time for it to be successful. He was obliged to follow strategic and tactical policies that were not remotely suited to the situation. The belief that the material production on the Malayan Peninsula, as well as the prestigious naval base and vital commercial facilities of Singapore, could be only protected by maintaining a strong air force may have been well founded, but that forced Percival to scatter his troops to protect the airfields. However, the airfields were only valuable if there was an adequate supply of modern fighter aircraft and pilots to fly them. Neither of these were to be had in 1941.

The absolute and wilful blindness in Whitehall and the British Army on the question of armoured vehicles was another problem. Simply assuming that the terrain was unsuitable for armoured warfare did not make it so. It was certainly true that tanks would struggle to cope with jungle and swamps or oil palm and rubber

43. Rice country in eastern Malaya. Far from being covered by 'impenetrable jungle', a great deal of 1940s Malaya was agricultural land. (Author's collection)

plantations, but the reality is that tanks mostly stick to roads, and without a good road system the produce of Malaya could not have been transported to Singapore for export around the world. Percival's problems did not stop there. A powerful belief on the part of various individuals in the civil authority that the Japanese would never attack impeded any progress toward an adequate civil defence policy. Similarly, a refusal to offer a living wage for local labour meant that very little was done to prepare defences in Singapore. The policy of defending the Singapore naval base continued to be a factor in Percival's planning, even when there were no ships left for the base to tend.

That said, Percival did make his own difficulties. He could and should have made much stronger representations for an allocation of tanks. Vehicles that were being relegated to training-only status in Britain – or even being consigned to scrap metal – might not have made the difference between ultimate defeat and victory, but with no tanks at all Malaya Command was virtually guaranteed to struggle against the Japanese. Percival also failed to ensure any viable degree of training at battalion or formation level. A small number of units – notably the Argylls – had been put through extensive training programmes by their commanding officers, but nothing was done to encourage this. At the level of brigades, divisions and corps there was virtually no training at all, which proved to be disastrous once the battle had been joined. Withdrawing in front of a determined enemy calls for a high level of competence and confidence at formation headquarters, which was conspicuous by its absence throughout the campaign. Percival repeatedly failed to replace senior officers who had been found wanting, though a decent training programme would probably have revealed some of the weaker officers and improved the understanding and competence of others. Throughout the Malayan campaign Percival was continually driven by two conflicting policies. On the one hand there was the need to retain territory, and on the other to preserve his army for what he called 'the main battle', which he envisaged fighting in northern Johore.

These two considerations were incompatible with one another. If he pursued a policy of fighting the Japanese at every turn his units would become depleted and exhausted; if he made a major withdrawal the Japanese would pursue him so rapidly that he would not be able to deploy his formations into a well-organised defensive structure before the enemy was upon them. Equally, he did not appear to give any real thought to countering the Japanese by attacking them in order to disrupt their advance, and very little effort was made to form sabotage parties behind their lines. Additionally, he put too much faith in blocking roads and demolishing bridges. A great many bridges were blown – sometimes leaving large bodies of troops and vital materiel on the wrong side of a river – but in virtually every instance the engineers of the Japanese Army proved capable of making repairs at such speed that the advance was seldom impeded for very long. Percival was undoubtedly influenced by his own combat experience in the First World War – during which he displayed conspicuous gallantry – and had far too strong a belief in the power of trenches and fixed defences long after they had proven unsound against the Japanese Army.

The failure of the Allies in Malaya and Singapore was not simply a matter of Percival's weaknesses as a commander, but he has 'carried the can' for the behaviour of others – notably the civil administration from Whitehall downwards – for seventy years.

If Percival was a 'loser' in 1942, General Bennett was most certainly a 'winner' on a personal level. Having failed time and again to make good decisions in Malaya – even when his troops performed admirably – Bennett continued in a similar vein in Singapore. His decision to do nothing when Brigadier Maxwell misconstrued his orders and withdrew from the Jurong Line, thereby destroying what little hope remained of turning the tide of the battle, is incomprehensible as well as unforgiveable. Not content with tactical ineptitude and a famous inability to get on with his commander, his colleagues or his subordinates, Bennett escaped – or rather ran away – from Singapore and made his way to Australia. Once there, he contrived to appear as something of a hero despite deserting his post and his men, and also managed to set himself up as an expert in jungle warfare.

Fruits of Victory?

The fruits of victory were immense, though not all of them could be put to immediate use. The great naval base that had cost so much money before the war, and the defence of which had been the primary purpose of the campaign waged by Percival, had not been subject to a comprehensive plan of destruction to deny it to the enemy – though it certainly should have been. However, it had not been captured intact and a great deal of work would be required to make it capable of supporting the sort of grand fleet that the Japanese would require to safeguard their new imperial domain.

Victory in Malaya and Singapore gave a tremendous boost to the prestige of the Japanese Army and Navy, and damaged Allied morale in other theatres. It brought great prestige to General Yamashita who had been somewhat out of favour in the years before the war. It also enhanced the reputation of Colonel Tsuji, who had planned the invasion. After the war he escaped prosecution as a war criminal, probably with the connivance of American and British authorities as part of their drive against communism, and eventually became a member of the Japanese post-war parliament. General Yamashita, on the other hand, went to the scaffold, though the war crimes evidence against him personally was patchy at best and his execution was probably more a product of the fact that he had defeated the British and the Australians than anything else. It may be argued that Yamashita could have imposed a tighter rein on his troops after the surrender and thereby have prevented the vast, wanton tide of murder, rape, brutality and robbery that swept through Singapore, but the reality is that anyone – soldier or civilian – engaged in such a horror is responsible for their own actions. There is a whiff of racism about Yamashita's prosecution;

had he been a German or Italian general it seems unlikely that he would have been hanged. In the end, the 'Tiger of Malaya' (as he was described in Japanese newspapers and propaganda material) was one of the losers. Yamashita was posted to Manchuria after the fall of Singapore and it is difficult to assess the extent of his real culpability for the events that followed the capitulation. He certainly failed to keep control of his troops, but it is impossible to make a clear distinction between the reaction of troops who have just completed a difficult campaign and the general ethos of the Japanese Army in the 1930s and 1940s. Japanese soldiers were themselves treated with exceptional brutality and had been indoctrinated to believe that surrender was unthinkable and that soldiers who did so rather than dying at their posts did not deserve to be treated in a humane way. Equally, Yamashita was not content to ignore their depredations. He ensured that a number of looters and the officer who led the infamous massacre at the Alexandra Hospital were executed and he made a personal apology to those patients who had survived.

Yamashita's troops remained in South East Asia after the capitulation. The Twenty-Fifth Army headquarters was moved to Bukit Tinggi in Sumatra and served as the occupying force there until the end of the war.

The fall of Singapore gave Japan undisputed access to the wealth of the whole of Malaya; particularly to tin and rubber, for which there was a huge worldwide market as well as enormous demand in Japan to support the war effort. Singapore itself was a great trophy. The significance as a financial centre was greatly reduced since she was no longer within the wider commercial sphere of the British Commonwealth. The huge Chinese financial industry was heavily undermined by the Japanese victory, partly because of the instability caused by the war, and partly because of the gigantic fines or 'contributions' that the Japanese demanded from the Chinese community. These removed so much liquid capital from the banks that it was almost impossible to pursue any sort of major commercial activity.

Colonel Masanobu Tsuji

Born in 1901 or 1902, Colonel Tsuji served in the Imperial Army from 1924–45. He was a staff officer in the Kwantung Army between 1937 and 1939, and was one of the officers who helped to bring about the events of the late 1930s. He was the chief planner of the Malayan invasion, making several reconnaissance flights before the war. He later wrote a book on the topic, *Singapore: The Japanese Version*, which sold well in Britain, Australia and the United States as well as in Japan.

Tsuji was a violent racist and was instrumental in numerous war atrocities – including the mass murder of Chinese civilians in the Sook Ching massacres after the fall of Singapore and the execution of American prisoners of war in the Philippines. He was personally fearless and was wounded in action several times. Despite his well-known participation in and even instigation of war crimes, Colonel Tsuji was able to escape prosecution by fleeing to Thailand in 1945, probably with the help of the British and American intelligence services, which hoped that men like Tsuji, with strong nationalistic, right-wing views, would be useful in preventing the rise of communism in Japan after the war. When it became clear that he, like so many other Japanese war criminals, would not be pursued, he returned to Japan, entered politics and was elected to the Diet – Japan's parliament. On one occasion he allegedly ate the liver of an Allied pilot who had been shot down during the Burma campaign and criticised his colleagues for refusing to join him in the meal. He disappeared during a trip to Laos in 1961 and was declared legally dead in 1968.

The business community throughout Malaya as a whole had been dislocated by a number of factors, many dependent on, but not limited to, the direct effects of combat. A large proportion of the managers, engineers and other professionals – both British and Asian – on whom the rubber and tin industries depended had left their posts. Many of the younger British professionals had been members of reserve and volunteer units and had been called up for active service immediately after the initial Japanese landings at Singora and Kota Bahru. Others had made their way to Singapore as the Japanese advanced down the peninsula. Many families had made the trip south to Singapore in the hope that the Japanese would be repelled in short order and that they would be able to return to their homes before too long, an attitude that persisted for some time due to the shameless manipulation of the press; the British authorities continually failed to allow accurate reporting of the Japanese advance. A consequence of this was that there was a degree of pressure on civilians not to take the opportunity to leave Singapore for Australia or Europe because they would be 'letting the side down'. Tens of thousands of civilians interned by the Japanese in February 1942 would suffer a brutal captivity for the next three and half years. Thousands of them died from neglect and cruelty and all of them would be scarred by the experience – some of them still suffer today.

Prisoners of War

When Percival surrendered he still had something in the region of 80,000 men under his command. This presented the Japanese with a problem. They had not envisaged having to deal with a body of prisoners of war that was larger than their own army. During the First World War some German service personnel – mostly sailors – had been prisoners of the Japanese and had been well-treated, but the situation was very different in 1942. Some Japanese – and a few British and Australians – assumed that the defeat of the Allies across South Asia and the Pacific would result in an armistice and peace conference within a matter of months, and that the POWs would be repatriated. This was hardly a realistic prospect so long as Japan was allied with Germany, and so long as Germany was at war with the Allies, but it would also have been an admission on the part of the British and the Dutch that their days as colonial powers in Asia had come to an end. Although Percival had sought and received assurances from Yamashita that the POWs – and the civilian population too – would be well treated, the reality was that Japan was not a signatory to the various conventions and agreements relating to military prisoners.

Yamashita was posted to Manchuria and replaced General Shimpei Fukuye, whose attitude toward the POWs was one of indifference at best and outright cruelty at worst. The POWs now became a pool of slave labour subjected to horrific conditions. To some extent, this was a product of the general ethos of the Japanese Army; beatings were a normal part of the training system to the extent that two recruits might be ordered to beat one another senseless for minor infractions. There was also a class and racial pecking order at work within the Japanese Army and in their attitude to prisoners. Essentially, officers were seen as being superior to NCOs socially as well as professionally and NCOs as superior to privates, but all Japanese saw themselves as racially superior to the many Korean troops in the Imperial Army and they in turn regarded themselves as racially superior to Chinese, Malays, Indians and Europeans. The combination of these attitudes, with a belief that an able-bodied man who surrendered was an affront to the traditions of soldiering and an embarrassment to his country, led to the institutionalised cruelty suffered by thousands of British, Australian and Indian soldiers from February 1942 to September 1945. Additionally, the sheer number of POWs was more than the Japanese administration could cope with. Huge numbers were sent to Japan to work in mines or on the infamous Burma Railway, or to build airstrips in the South Pacific. Thousands died from disease, malnutrition and abuse; thousands more were simply shot out of hand when they had outlived their immediate usefulness.

A great many Indian soldiers endured the captivity despite having an opportunity to return to the front as soldiers of the Japanese Imperial Army. In the months after the surrender, the Japanese formed the *Azad Hind Fauj* or Indian National Army (INA), supposedly a force raised to fight the British to achieve Indian independence, but essentially a means of raising Indian troops for the campaign in Burma. The INA recruited about 12,000 men, less than one in four of the Indian POWs in Malaya. The remarkable thing is that so few volunteered. Many Indian troops felt – with some justice – that they had been abandoned by the British. Many had received very little training and there was at least one incident of a European – presumed to be British – addressing Indian prisoners and telling them that the Japanese were now their masters and should be obeyed. The first attempt to raise the INA force was undermined by a belief that the Japanese intention was not to liberate India from the British, but to take control themselves. However, a second attempt to raise an Indian force was more successful and by the end of the war there were over 30,000 men in the INA. Many of the prisoners, especially those who were career soldiers, remained loyal to the British Crown only to find that when India became independent they were denied their pension rights, so they must surely be counted among the 'losers' of the Malayan campaign.

Occupation

The Japanese occupation of Singapore and Malaya proved to be a period of misery and terror for the local civilian population. Some portions of the community suffered more than others – especially the Chinese – but a mixture of rapaciousness, neglect and administrative mismanagement in every field led to starvation and disease, and a well-founded fear of the unpredictability of the occupation forces generally and of the *Kempeitai* in particular. The latter was essentially a department within the army but charged with a wide variety of roles, including intelligence, counter-intelligence and imposing Japanese authority on the residents of occupied territories through sheer terror. Another factor was the Sook Ching massacres in which thousands of Singaporeans (mostly Chinese) were summarily murdered by the Japanese Army in mass shootings and drownings. The Sook Ching operation (the Japanese called the process *Kakyoshukusei* or 'the purging of Chinese') was a deliberately planned policy of mass murder, which theoretically focused on specific groups in the Chinese community, though a great many people were selected and executed at random. The primary targets of Sook Ching included members of the Overseas Chinese Anti-Japanese Army. Known as Dalforce, the unit – about 500 strong – had been formed by Lieutenant Colonel John Dalley of the Federated Malay States Police Force on Christmas Day 1941 and had fought valiantly in defence of Singapore. Other target groups included those who had been active in or contributors to the China Relief Fund (an organisation that raised money for the struggle against the Japanese in China), civil servants, members of the Singapore Legislative Council, people from Hainan who were assumed to be communists and men with tattoos who were assumed to be gangsters. The Sook Ching massacres are relatively well known, but random shootings and beheadings in the street were a common sight throughout the occupation, particularly in the first few weeks after the surrender.

The bombing and shelling of the campaign caused extensive damage to commerce and manufacturing across Singapore, which was exacerbated by a policy of destroying goods and installations to deny them to the Japanese. Economic dislocation throughout Malaya – particularly in the vital rubber, tin and palm oil industries – was further exacerbated because many Chinese and Indian business people from mainland Malaya, especially those who had been involved in fundraising activities to support the struggle against Japan in China, had travelled to Singapore to avoid capture. Once there, most of them discovered that they could not get on a ship to Australia or India since the available transport was almost exclusively reserved for Europeans; however, their absence

SOOK CHING

Sook Ching was a mass-murder operation conducted by the Japanese military secret police and army under Lieutenant Colonel Masayuki Oishi. It was conducted over three weeks in the immediate aftermath of the surrender of Singapore. The operation had been planned in the weeks immediately prior to the attack on Singapore and the carefully targeted victims included wealthy men and women who had given or raised funds for arms and supplies used to resist the Japanese invasion of China, communists, trade unionists, Chinese cultural activists of all kinds and people who just happened to be prominent in the community. Colonel Tsuji, chief planner of the Malaya invasion, urged that the Sook Ching exercise be extended to the mainland and thousands of Chinese people were executed – at random mostly – through the length and breadth of the country.

from their factories and mines meant that production was hampered or even stopped entirely. Consequently, workers were not receiving wages, which had a knock-on effect on virtually every business and shop in the country.

The productivity of Malaya was impaired by the absence of these people, but not irretrievably. The policy of denial was not as effective in Singapore as it might have been, but on the mainland there had been no real effort to put together any sort of general plan to prevent industrial and commercial facilities from falling to the Japanese. This was largely a product of unrealistic policies – indeed, little more than a chronic attack of wishful thinking – on the part of the British authorities. A policy of destroying factories and processing facilities would have been an admission that the Japanese advance could not be resisted and that the Allies had no prospect of driving the Japanese back out again. Additionally, there was the question of compensation: if or when the Japanese were defeated, who would pay for installations and stocks that had been destroyed to keep them out of enemy hands?

The Japanese had acquired the wealth of Malaya and Singapore and, therefore, denied it to the British. The rubber and tin that were so important to the production of munitions were also in demand all around the world and their loss was a great blow to Britain's economy.

For the Japanese, the economic value of victory was vast, but there was also a political value. By defeating the British and the Australians, her forces had undermined widely held views on racial superiority and she had established herself as a major modern power on the world stage. She now became the dominant force throughout South and East Asia at the expense of the European countries – Britain, France and the Netherlands – and she had made a start on achieving a similar position as the dominant force in the Pacific at the expense of the United States. Japan had exposed the British political and military structures in Asia as weak and inflexible. The much-vaunted slogan of 'Asia for the Asians' and the concept of the greater Asian Co-Prosperity Sphere may have been quickly revealed as simple Japanese imperialism, but it had certainly shown that the Europeans generally and the British in particular were far from invincible, and that the continuation of their rule in Asia, regardless of the outcome of the war, was by no means assured.

For the people of Malaya and Singapore, the British had been replaced by a far more oppressive source of authority and in the early months of 1942, as communities adjusted to the new dispensation, it must have seemed very doubtful that any power on earth would be able to liberate them; Japan had triumphed. In reality, her position was far from secure. Japan's attack on Pearl Harbor pushed Hitler into declaring war on America. Over the next two years the United States would become the world's greatest industrial power, and American materiel and manpower would be instrumental in bringing down Nazi Germany and then imperial Japan little more than three years after the fall of Singapore.

The people of Malaya and Singapore were certainly losers in any economic, political or social sense, but the British had suffered an enormous military and political defeat. Percival's surrender

44. One British pre-war banknote and three Japanese 'Occupation' currency banknotes. The Japanese banknotes lost their value very quickly during the occupation years. (Author's collection)

gave the Japanese credibility as a military power and brought a considerable prize in military materiel. Huge quantities of small arms, artillery and, perhaps most importantly, vehicles fell into Japanese hands just at the point when Japanese industry was really starting to struggle with the demands made by the army and navy.

Final Effects

Defeat in Malaya and Singapore was a huge blow to British prestige abroad and, for a while, undermined confidence at home because so much had been made of the 'impregnability' of 'Fortress Singapore'. The failure to defeat the Japanese either in Malaya or Burma was unsettling to Britain's new ally, the United States. Although American public and political opinion was much more focused on the attacks on Pearl Harbor and in the Philippines, the fact that a very large British force had been comprehensively defeated by a smaller one in only ten weeks did nothing to aid American confidence in the British military establishment.

In the short term, the Japanese Empire was certainly the beneficiary of the campaign. Their successes in late 1941 and early 1942 made a great impression on their Axis allies. Strategically, however, the fall of Malaya eased some of the burden on the Royal Navy who could now devote more resources to the Atlantic and to ensuring supplies to the British Army and the RAF who, in turn, could now concentrate more effectively on the campaigns in North Africa and Burma though the latter continued to be at the end of the queue for resources. The victory of the Japanese Army and Navy in Malaya was total and crushing in both a strategic and tactical sense, though in terms of grand strategy and policy, the acquisition of the vast territory conquered in 1941–42 made them as vulnerable as the British, Dutch and Americans had been when hostilities opened, and in fact they adopted a very similar policy to that of the British before the war. Essentially, the rationale was that although Japan now had an enormous perimeter to defend, it would take the Allies a long time to deliver a counter-offensive and that wherever they chose to strike there would be ample time for Japan to mount a relief operation strong enough to destroy any Allied expeditionary force.

In practice, the Japanese really had to fight several very different wars at the same time and had seriously underestimated the capacities of their enemies. By the summer of 1945 the emperor's forces had been defeated in Burma, New Guinea and the South Pacific. Japan's war industries were collapsing and her manpower shortage was critical, but she still had extensive commitments throughout South and East Asia. By September 1945 the Allies were ready to invade Malaya (Operation Zipper) with an overwhelming force of British, Indian and African troops who had more than got the measure of the Japanese in every aspect of combat and had successfully driven them from Burma. Only the atomic attacks on Hiroshima and Nagasaki prevented a hard and bloody campaign to liberate Malaya and Singapore from what had been an incredibly brutal Japanese occupation. At the time it was not absolutely clear that even those attacks were sufficient to end the war in the Far East. Field Marshal Terauchi seems to have been willing to fight to the bitter end and might well have done so had he not fallen victim to a heart attack.

In one sense, the 'winners' of the Malayan campaign included British politicians of the 1920s and 1930s and of the wartime coalition government. The British political establishment had failed miserably to ensure the security of either the various colonial possessions or the different states whose defence had been promised in treaties. None of the political figures were held to account after the war. Churchill's promise that there would be an inquiry as soon as war was over and all relevant persons available to give evidence was not kept. In part this was due to the change of government in the 1945 General Election, but of course several members of that government had also been members of the wartime coalition Cabinet. Letting the matter fade into obscurity was in the interests of senior politicians of both the Conservative and Labour Parties, since so many of them would have had hard questions to answer had it not.

THE LEGACY

For the British there was a very real military legacy from the Malayan campaign. Defeat led to the creation of specialist warfare schools, and within a remarkably short space of time the British became remarkably good jungle soldiers and the value of the tank in tropical climates had been amply proven. Both of these factors were crucial aspects of the campaign to liberate Burma from Japanese occupation. In turn, long-range jungle operations led to great strides in the development of techniques for re-supply by air.

The political legacy of the fall of Singapore in 1942 can be read in a number of ways. For the British and Singaporeans alike it was the beginning of the end for a colonial relationship that had its origins in the trading adventures of the East India Company more than a century before. There is a very positive social, cultural and commercial legacy which continues to this day. There is probably no other former British colony where British visitors are more welcome than they are in Singapore. Restoration of British rule in 1945 was a relatively easy process, but the Japanese invasion and occupation had encouraged the view that Malaya, Singapore and all the other European colonies should start to decide their own destiny. The occupation had been brutal in the extreme. Estimates vary, but perhaps a quarter, possibly even one-third of Singapore's population lost their lives under the Japanese. If the British could guarantee security there was a lot to be said for independence. In 1948 a new conflict – known as the Malayan Emergency – broke out between the British authorities and the Malayan Communist Party (MCP). By the time the Emergency was over, Malaysia and Singapore had achieved independence, but not through the activities of the MCP, who had been beaten so comprehensively that Britain was able to deliver a degree of autonomy to Singapore in 1955 and independence for Malaya in 1957. The MCP had been established before the war, but had always been essentially a Chinese organisation. Malays and Indians – or Europeans for that matter – were not formally excluded, but were not particularly welcome in its ranks.

The Japanese threat to British rule in the Far East was largely, but not totally, ignored in the period before the invasion. In August 1941 the 'Oriental Mission' of the Special Operations Executive (SOE) tried to start a department in Singapore with a view to recruiting and training a resistance force in the event of a Japanese invasion, but were prevented from making any progress – partly because few people believed that Japan was a threat at all, but largely through the obstruction of Sir Shenton Thomas, the Governor of the Straits Settlements. As the campaign came to a close the MCP became the foundation of the Malayan People's Anti-Japanese Army (MPAJA). Largely Chinese and communist, the MPAJA was the main body of armed resistance to the occupation and had some contact with British missions mounted by Force 136, the operational cover name for the SOE. The line between the MPAJA and the various bandit groups that had existed before the war was often hazy, but operations were mounted, sabotage was carried out, Japanese soldiers were killed and the MPAJA gained some credibility.

When the Emergency started in 1948 the MCP took their arms out of storage, erected camps in inaccessible jungle and mountain areas and started a 'war of independence', adopting the title of the 'Malayan People's Liberation Army' (MPLA). Under the command of Chin Peng – a former leader of the MPAJA who had been decorated by the British for his actions against the Japanese

– the MPLA grew to a strength of about 13,000 at its peak, but never seriously threatened British rule. As it became increasingly clear that the British had no intention of retaining a permanent hold over Malaya, it became harder for the MPLA to gather recruits or supplies and by 1955 the British government was able to offer an amnesty to MPLA members.

During the occupation years, the Japanese had adopted a 'divide and rule' policy, which encouraged racial tensions which would continue to trouble Malaysia intermittently for decades. Tension had already existed between the Chinese immigrants and the indigenous population. The Chinese had largely come to Malaya to work either in tin or in business or the professions and were seen as profiting at the expense of the Malays. A similar tension existed between Malays, the Chinese and the Indian community, most of whom had come to Malaya to work in British concerns or in the police force or army.

In every sense, the victory of the Japanese Empire in Malaya and the fall of Singapore was an immense blow to the credibility and prestige of the British government. At the most immediate level, the arms, doctrine and leadership of the British Army – and therefore of the Commonwealth forces – had proved unequal to the task of seriously impeding, let alone repelling, an invasion by a force of significantly smaller numbers equipped with materiel that was far from being 'state of the art' by the standards of 1941–42. The loss of manpower and materiel was immense: a total of 80,000 men had been taken prisoner; the Japanese had captured hundreds of guns, thousands of vehicles, tens of thousands of small arms and massive quantities of ammunition and other supplies. They had also captured the great Singapore naval base, which had cost many millions of pounds to build but had made no real contribution to the defence of the empire. The base was of precious little value unless there was a powerful fleet for it to support, but that fleet had failed to materialise due to the extensive demands on the Royal Navy in the Atlantic, the Mediterranean, the Indian Ocean and the defence of home waters.

Once Singapore fell there was no realistic prospect of containing the Japanese advance in the Dutch East Indies, which had been invaded on 10 January 1942, so the defeat of the British had a detrimental effect on the credibility of the Netherlands as a colonial power. In contrast to Malaya, the Japanese were, initially, widely welcomed by the local population. The claim that Japan was liberating Asia from the European colonialists initially found more fertile ground in the Dutch East Indies than anywhere else, but soon wore very thin. The Japanese did, however, rely heavily on local administrators who took the place of the Dutch civilians who had been sent to internment camps. Under the Japanese, local leaders who gained the approval of the occupation government were able to build relationships with the people and thus develop a political community that was opposed to the restoration of Dutch rule. Additionally, the Japanese provided arms and training for locally recruited men, so when the war ended in August 1945 there was a well-developed independence movement that could not only declare its independence from the Netherlands, but had an armed force to back up its position. The result was a struggle between the nationalists eager to achieve independence and the Dutch government who were equally eager to retain control over the valuable rubber and oil industries. The war continued for more than four years, but the result was never really in doubt. Even before the Japanese invasion it was clear to many that the age of European colonial rule in South Asia was not going to last forever. However, the campaign of 1941–42 certainly accelerated the process by demonstrating that the British, the Dutch and the French in Indo-China were not invincible and that colonial rule was, therefore, not inevitable.

Once the mineral and produce wealth of South Asia was in Japanese hands, oil, tin, rubber and foodstuffs could be channelled into the imperial war effort. More than that, Japan's military and industrial resources could be focused on the pursuit of campaigns in other theatres. Men, tanks and aircraft could be transferred to the war against the British and the Chinese in Burma – with the prospect that it might be possible to make an incursion into India which could destabilise British rule. Assets could be transferred to the Pacific campaign against the Americans and to press the war in China. The southern front might in due course be extended to Australia and, though the prospect of actually conquering Australia might be beyond practical expectations, it would not be impossible for the Japanese high command to think that they might be able to force Australia to seek terms. That in turn would have implications for the British war effort in the desert, as well as removing the Royal Australian Navy from an active role in the Indian Ocean and in the Pacific.

Defeat at Singapore was a blow to the prestige of Churchill's government at home as well, and not just among those with relatives and friends – civil as well as military – who had now become prisoners. Had the British populace been aware of the conditions that the prisoners would suffer, the situation would have been that much worse. Singapore was only one of a number of disasters: the fall of Hong Kong, the retreat through Burma and the mixed fortunes of war in North Africa had been preceded by a veritable litany of failure in France, Flanders and Norway. The matter of Singapore was made worse by the fact that the government – and the military – had been so eager to portray the Far East imperial possessions as secure and Singapore itself as impregnable.

The shock was felt throughout British society, but it had an effect on the general prestige of the British Empire right around the world, in the United States, Canada and – for obvious reasons – in Australia. In occupied Europe it helped to make the prospect of an eventual triumph over the Nazis seem much less likely.

Most importantly, the defeat of British arms spelt the beginning of the end for the security of British rule in South Asia and, indeed, anywhere else. In the past it had seemed that a benefit of British rule was military protection and the British had now failed utterly to live up to their obligations. Certainly, the British had a vast range of commitments elsewhere, but that was of little comfort to people who now faced indefinite occupation by Japan.

Failure in Singapore cast a very long shadow. Twenty years later, when the threat came from Indonesia rather than Japan, Singaporeans might have asked, 'What will you British do if the Indonesians invade? Will you run away again ... like when the Japanese came?' This was not altogether a fair assessment, but it was understandable.

The wider point of course is that since Britain had proved incapable of defending her eastern possessions, those possessions would, eventually, have to defend themselves, which would render an imperial relationship unsustainable and independence inevitable. Britain's withdrawal from empire did not follow a particularly rational path. Notionally, the retention of the Singapore naval base, several RAF and army establishments and even the construction of the new Royal Marines barracks at Nee Soon as late as the 1960s were functions of the need to preserve the trade routes of the empire and Commonwealth, and to maintain the prestige of Britain as a world-class power. Neither policy really made much sense. Britain could not possibly sustain the level of spending required to keep abreast of conventional military advances, support establishments around the world and develop a nuclear capacity. When the wartime legacy of National Service came to an end, voluntary enlistment could not provide the necessary manpower to maintain a large field army in Germany in addition to commitments in Asia, Africa and South America. The political picture was changing as well. At the end of the Second World War Britain had decided not to become part of the movement toward the economic integration that would eventually become the European Union, but was clearly headed that way by the 1960s.

As British interests became more closely aligned with mainland Europe, Singapore and Malaya became more focused on the fast-developing Asian and Australian markets, but had a difficult relationship. In 1963 Malaya, Singapore, Sabah, Brunei and Sarawak united into a federal state to be known as Malaysia. The marriage was not a happy one. The central government adopted policies of affirmative action to improve the standing of the Malay population, which – rightly or wrongly – were seen as discriminating against Chinese and Indian citizens. By 1965 disagreements between the federal government and the state government in Singapore had become so marked that the Malaysian parliament voted unanimously to expel Singapore from Malaysia. Although the Prime Minister of Singapore, Lee Kuan Yew, had been a strong advocate of the union with Malaya, by 1965 he too had become convinced that the experiment was failing and on 9 August Singapore became an independent republic. The situation was not propitious since Malaysia, and now the new republic of Singapore, were engaged in the 'Confrontation' with Indonesia, a conflict which has received little attention from historians. The Indonesian government had not been strongly opposed to the creation of Malaysia, but had changed its position on the grounds that it was no more than a political front to disguise continuing British control in South Asia.

Indonesia had recently gained control of the former Netherlands colony of West Papua and it is possible that President Sukarno hoped to acquire Sarawak, Sabah and even Singapore by force of arms. Although he was well aware of the extent of British military assets in the region, Sukarno was not convinced that the British government would be prepared to wage a war to protect Malaysia or Singapore, and may have believed that the experience of 1941–42 indicated that they could not do so successfully. What he may not have seen is that the experience had helped to encourage the people of Malaya and Singapore to reject colonialism from any source whatsoever.

ORDERS OF BATTLE

Japanese Order of Battle

Twenty-Fifth Army (GOC Gen. Yamashita)

18th Division (Lt Gen. Renya Mutaguchi)
23rd Infantry Brigade
114th Infantry Regiment
A detachment of 1st Independent Anti-Tank Battalion
18th Mountain Artillery Regiment
21st Heavy Field Artillery Battalion
12th Engineer Regiment
Engineer Unit of 21st Independent Brigade and 3rd Field Hospital
23rd Independent Engineer Regiment (attached)
15th River Crossing Company (attached)
22nd Bridge Building Material Company (attached)

5th Division (Lt Gen. Takuro Matsui)
21st Infantry Brigade
2nd Independent Anti-Tank Company
One medium tank company
5th Field Artillery Regiment
5th Engineer Regiment

9th Infantry Brigade
1st Independent Anti-Tank Company
15th Independent Engineer Regiment (attached)
A detachment of the engineering unit of 3rd Tank Group (attached)
21st River Crossing Material Company (attached)
27th Bridge Building Material Company (attached)
58th Construction Duty Company (attached)
26th Independent Engineering Company (attached)
41st Infantry Regiment (reserve)
5th Reconnaissance Regiment (reserve)
14th Independent Mortar Company (reserve)
1st Tank Regiment (reserve)
2nd Field Hospital (reserve)
4th Field Hospitals (reserve)

Imperial Guards Division (Lt Gen. Takuma Nishimura)
3rd Battalion, 4th Guards Infantry Regiment
3rd Guards Infantry Regiment
3rd Guards Anti-Tank and Regimental Artillery Units
Two companies of 1st Independent Anti-Tank Battalion
One company of Guards Engineer Regiment
A medical unit
2nd Battalion, 5th Guards Infantry Regiment
Regimental Artillery Company
Regimental Anti-Tank Company
14th Tank Regiment
Two companies of the Guards Reconnaissance Regiment
Guards Artillery Regiment (support)
20th Independent Engineer Regiment (attached)
One company from 26th Independent Engineers Regiment (attached)
5th Guards Regiment (reserve)

Commonwealth Order of Battle

The field army that was available to General Percival at the beginning of the campaign consisted of the two divisions of III Indian Corps under Lt Gen. Heath, the two brigades of 8th Australian Division under Maj. Gen. Bennett and one independent infantry brigade under Brigadier Paris. In the last weeks of the campaign Percival received reinforcements in considerable number, including 44th and 45th Indian Brigades, 7,000 Indian and 1,900 Australian replacements, 2/14th Australian Machine Gun Battalion and, on 29 January, the British 18th Division.

Malaya Command (GOC Lt Gen. Percival)

Singapore Fortress (Maj. Gen. Keith Simmons)
1st Malaya Brigade (Brig. G.G.R. Williams)
2nd Battalion, Loyals
1st Battalion, Malay Regiment
2nd Malaya Brigade (Brig. F.H. Fraser)
1st Battalion, Manchester Regiment
2nd Battalion, Gordon Highlanders
1/7th Dogras

Coast and Anti-Aircraft Artillery

7th Coast Regiment
9th Coast Regiment
16th Defence Regiment
35th Fortress Company
41st Fortress Company
3rd Heavy AA Regiment
1st Heavy AA Regiment (HKSRA)
2nd Heavy AA Regiment (HKSRA)
3rd Light AA Regiment (HKSRA)
1st AA Regiment, Indian Artillery

5th S/L Regiment, Jind Infantry ISF
Kapurthala Infantry ISF

III Indian Corps (Lt Gen. Sir Lewis Heath)
11th Indian Division (Maj. Gen. D. Murray-Lyon)
    3rd Cavalry
    137th Field Regiment
    155th Field Regiment
    80th Anti-Tank Regiment
    23rd Field Company, Sappers and Miners
    43rd Field Park Company

6th Indian Brigade (Brig. W.O. Lay)
    22nd Mountain Regiment
    17th Field Company, Sappers and Miners
    2nd Battalion East Surreys
    1/8th Punjab
    2/16th Punjab

15th Indian Infantry Brigade (Brig. K.A. Garret)
    3rd Field Company, Sappers and Miners
    1st Battalion Leicester Regiment
    2/9th Jats
    1/14th Punjab
    3/16th Punjab

9th Indian Division (Maj. Gen. A.E. Barstow)

8th Indian Infantry Brigade (Brig. B.W. Key)
    21st Mountain Battery
    19th Field Company, Sappers and Miners
    2/10th Baluchi
    3/17th Dogras
    1/13th Frontier Force Rifles

22nd Indian Infantry Brigade (Brig. G.W.A. Painter)
  21st Mountain Artillery
  22nd Field Company, Sappers and Miners
  5/11th Sikhs
  2/18th Royal Garwhal Rifles
  2/12th Frontier Force Regiment

Penang Fortress (Brig. C.A. Lyon)
  11th Coast Regiment
  35th Fortress Company
  5/14th Punjab

Airfield Defence Troops
  1st Bahawalpur Infantry ISF
  1st Hyderabad Infantry ISF
  1st Mysore Infantry ISF

28th Indian Infantry Brigade (Brig. W. St J. Carpendale)
  2/1st Ghurkha Rifles
  2/2nd Ghurkha Rifles
  2/9th Ghurkha Rifles

12th Indian Infantry Brigade (Brig. A.C.M. Paris)
  122th Field Regiment
  15th Field Company, Sappers and Miners
  2nd Battalion, Argyll and Sutherland Highlanders
  5/2nd Punjab
  4/19th Hyderabad

8th Australian Division (Maj. Gen. H.G. Bennett)

2/10th Field Regiment
2/15th Field Regiment
4th Anti-Tank Regiment
2/10th Field Company

2/12th Field Company
2/6th Field Park Company

22nd Australian Infantry Brigade (Brig. H.B. Taylor)
      2/18th Battalion
      2/19th Battalion
      2/20th Battalion

27th Australian Infantry Brigade (Brig. D.S. Maxwell)
      2/26th Battalion
      2/29th Battalion
      2/30th Battalion

18th British Division (Maj. Gen. M.B. Beckwith-Smith)

118th Field Regiment RA
135th Field Regiment RA
148th Field Regiment RA
125th Anti-Tank Regiment RA
287th Field Company RE
280th Field Company RE
560th Field Company RE
251st Field Park Company RE
9th Northumberland Fusiliers (Machine Gun Battalion)
18th Battalion
Reconnaissance Battalion

53rd Infantry Brigade (Brig. C.L.B. Duke)
      5th Battalion, Royal Norfolk
      8th Battalion, Royal Norfolk
      2nd Battalion, Cambridgeshire Regiment

54th Infantry Brigade (Brig. E.H.W. Backhouse)
      4th Battalion, Royal Norfolk
      4th Battalion, Suffolk Regiment
      5th Battalion, Suffolk Regiment

55th Infantry Brigade (Brig. T.H. Massy-Beresford)
        5th Battalion, Bedfordshire and Hertfordshire Regiment
        1/5th Sherwood Foresters
        1st Battalion, Cambridgeshire Regiment

FURTHER READING

Barber, Noel, *Sinister Twilight*, London, 1968.

Bennett, Henry G., *Why Singapore Fell*, Sydney, 1944.

Chippingto, George, *Singapore: The Inexcusable Betrayal*, Hanley Swann, 1992.

Cooper, Duff, *Old Men Forget*, London, 1954.

Elphick, Peter, *Singapore: The Pregnable Fortress*, London, 1995.

Percival, Arthur, *The War in Malaya*, London, 1949.

Owen, Frank, *The Fall of Singapore*, London, 1960.

Simson, Ivan, *Singapore: Too Little, Too Late*, London, 1970.

Thompson, Peter, *The Battle for Singapore*, London, 2005.

Tsuji, Masanobu, *Singapore: The Japanese Version*, London, 1966.

Woodburn Kirby, S., *The War Against Japan*, Vol. 1, London, 1957.

FEPOW: www.fepow.com has many links to very useful websites relating to the campaign.

Glasgow University is involved in The Adam Park Project, conducting battlefield archaeology.

Malayan Volunteers Group: www.malayanvolunteersgroup is an excellent source of material relating to volunteer units in the Malayan campaign.

The National Archives of Singapore has two websites: Memories of The Ford Factory and Reflections at Bukit Chandu.

INDEX